2012

WAKE UP

THE END IS NEAR

I hope this book inspires you to open your eyes for the coming of 2012. We're almost there. It will be a new time. The entire psychic is changing. We must purify our minds, body and soul.

We must elevate ourselves to be angelic. This age is going to be awareness and experience, and wisdom. Everything comes from one source, that source is God.

We are entering the Age of AQUARIUS. It will be the age of knowledge and faith and trust. It will only be for those who keep up. We will become united as one. A new beginning.

With the Age of Aquarius, everything will be different. Our world will be different. Politics, our nation, the land, and the boundaries will be different. Things will happen; changes are inevitable. We're living in a world disrupted by Planetary changes, Political wares while things are moving and shifting incredibly fast. We have to be stable to serve others. We have to touch every heart while we are here to make a change in this world.

We can change the world through our sustenance, grit, commitment, character, dignity, grace and radiance. We have to serve all over the world. We need to serve the global community now as everything is life. It all comes to pass.

The Aquarian age you don't pray. You ask God to pray for you. Tell God, "Lord pray for me that I should be infinite as you. Make me as bright, bountiful, and beautiful as you. Lord give me the power of love to serve. Let me know to serve myself, Let me touch and heal. Let my sight create miracles where I exist.

Forgive your environment and people.

Always repeat, "I am healthy. I am happy. I am holy."

Don't control the world. Control yourself.

Drink a cup of Joy. It is time to rejoice.

Forgive your past. Walk in the light. Ask your angels to guide you. It is time to Immerse Yourself within the Self.

We need people like the Gurus, Gandhi, the ARE Clinic, etc. to get others on the right track before 2011 and 2012.

Don't change the world. Change yourself.

God will supply you with everything you need. Love inspires and illumines and designates the way.

Everyday fill yourself with peace, love, joy, health and good thoughts.

If you want something, don't go to it. Let it come to you. If you keep trying, it is beyond reach.

Forget who you are. Reach out. Heal the world. When you heal someone else's problem, problems will disappear. God and the heavens will be kind to you.

2012
WAKE UP
THE END IS NEAR

Edgar Cayce

by Gayle Schilz

authorHOUSE®

AuthorHouse™
1663 Liberty Drive
Bloomington, IN 47403
www.authorhouse.com
Phone: 1-800-839-8640

First published by AuthorHouse   06/09/2011

ISBN: 978-1-4634-1889-2 (sc)
ISBN: 978-1-4634-1888-5 (ebk)

Printed in the United States of America

CONTENTS

ACKNOWLEDGEMENTS

I am dedicating this book to Edgar Cayce. With Great Respect And Love for this great being he was and is still coming to me though my dreams.

I woke up one morning and all I could think of was Edgar Cayce to write a book, the thoughts came to me about 2012, Wake Up the End is Near. As we will be guided into the new kingdom. But the greatest miracle is Unity. For the entire world Edgar Cayce did for others he is still coming through to us from the spirit world. His work does not end, as he was a great psychic and prophet.

I was cured of epilepsy through the Edgar Cayce handbook.

One of the apostles of Jesus had epilepsy, After he came out of the spell, he could predict the future.

I am truly grateful for a friend of mine who adopted me in her heart, brought me up with Edgar Cayce. She herself was psychic. She said she would come back to me through a trumpet She told me many things and wanted me to take over her readings. My ways are different than hers as she passed away. As she told me fifteen years before that President Richard M. Nixon would be impeached.

My deepest gratitude to those who came into my life and are still in my dreams.

I had the greatest parents in the world.

Right before my dad passed away he touched my face and a flash of light came into my head. As he was ready to leave this world. But I feel we are all connected in some way.

My mom and I were real close but a few days before she died you could her real faint that she was deleting everything she knew from the day she was born right up to the end. And her uncle Joe came and said he left but would be back.

The morning my mom passed away the nurse said your mom took her last breath. I stood up and felt this energy go through my body as she was leaving this earth planet. I'd had a wart on the bottom of my foot for three years and three different doctors could not get rid of it. I looked at my foot. The wart was gone. I felt cleansed insides.

I never knew what kind of life I would have but what ever happens, I just keep on going.

Through the Edgar Cayce ARE Clinic, with yoga, spiritual healing, staying on a spiritual path, and helping others, we can all make it and to face the challenges in life that presents us, no matter how hard it may seen as we can achieve our dreams. You have to find inner peace and strength within yourself.

Yoga over forty-five years, with meditation, hand mudras, therapeutic touching as well. I pray everyday for all those concerned.

I hope what else you do in life, do it with grace and love that this book will give you a more positive mental attitude to cope with your everyday experiences. May God fill your life with peace and love as he did mine. Don't change the world. Change yourself.

With Great Respect and Love,
Gayle

Epilepsy People with epilepsy understand it, but those that don't understand don't take the time to understand it. Some don't understand anything. Just plain ignorance!

My aunt had a daughter who was handicapped so I started volunteering at thirteen years old. My cousin passed away at sixty-two. At the funeral, I met a girl who was my cousin's friend. She was touching the coffin and said to her mother. I looked in your daughter's eyes. She is an old soul; she said yes, she had lived a thousand past lives. Then she told me they visit the ARE Clinic Edgar Cayce Foundation often.

I want to thank Steve and Kara Waddell and Joel.

AQUARIUS 2012

The Age of Aquarius is coming our way. We have to take away emptiness, insanity and pain for Judgment Day. We sit in this world. We have to remain disciplined in this disciplined world. We have to master ourselves. We need character commitment and grace. We have to overflow with energy, touch their hearts and fill this empty space.

Our action will be great. We will create a new humanity race. We want life to be right for all our children, for the whole society to find inner peace, to laugh and love and shine because life is only a lease on time and space.

So do your part and live in peace. Yet if this world would disappear from view, still it would always be the same.

CHAPTER 1

Prosperity

Attitude of Gratitude

You should take even a second when you listen and speak. In one second you can see the light and have total effectiveness than the third eye. Take this second to lift. It is the beaming of your command center. When people talk, listen. Stop for a second and answer. You'll be shocked how much you know.

Br grateful you are breathing and alive. So don't go and get it. Let it come to you.

"Character brings you prosperity."

Prosperity

"When people have calamity and misfortune—adversity. These three sisters come to visit who react to them. Opportunity, fortune, good luck are three sisters too, come to visit those who are calm, quiet and peaceful, that is inner tranquility.

You should live with kindness, compassion and serve. All this of all is knowledge, happiness, prosperity and richness.

"Serving is the only way to elevate your consciousness, Doing community service, *cloning* for others but doing something where there is no status, no reward. Your reward is hundred-thousand-fold from the heavens. It is called seeding the fortune."

God is always willing to give, but are we willing to receive?

When you cannot give then you can't progress. If you are scared, you are very insecure. Then you feel terrible and miserable. Then you live the rest of your life with a lot of pain.

We have so many environments of pressure: weight, value, status, and virtues. Then we suffer. The actual fact is we want to suffer. But if you relax, we could never suffer.

If you can take 11 minutes a day (mornings) it will help you to understand God—that God is the *Dole* of everything. "Let your energy flow."

"When you think of your child or his or her strength of tomorrow, think of that child as an angel or yourself. Never recognize your child. If you do not recognize the angel, you'll never recognize God."

Be healthy. Be happy. Be holy. There is no one on this planet who does not want to be Healthy, Happy and Holy . . . people carry the world in the palm of their hands.

Doing *kundalini* yoga is the reserve energy to open the light of God.

We're not here by any accident or incident. We're here to connect and join, or disconnect and lose. The hand of God, which created you, should carry you and will carry you if you let it be.

While you grow spiritually then we let everybody grow with us. Our words affect our hearts and bring confusion to clarity' then ill-health, then certain situations in life a place where we can understand how great it is to be healthy.

When you lean to a path of individual prosperity and spirituality and your surroundings are rich indeed, we should try to understand each other for we are here on this earth to visit.

People are struggling with their narrowness and shortcomings. They are confined to collect the weather. They are unhappy because someone else has what they want.

God is the one who manages and arranges the circumstances which simple therapy can help people.

There is a formula to help cleanse people's minds of parasites—which are called thoughts, miserable dirty thoughts, pounding humans. Cleansing ourselves of these parasites can be very difficult.

We may have guilt and try to get rid of that guilt but we can't and to try and save our own skins. But we forget God is with us all the time.

What we need to know is to understand the technology and psychology is the way to make a very small little being to a big vast being.

May we all live as a nation and understand life so we grow in this essence. Have peace and power of peace within you. Remember God is With Us. May we all live in piety and prosperity.

There is no room for doubt. Faith is an assumption. Faith is the assumption that the Universe will take care. It is the assumption which causes the effect. Envelop yourself in the gentle loving and abundant arms of the Universe. Allow yourself to be taken care of. May God bless you that the bounty of the Universe belongs to us all.

Never doubt. Change your negative thoughts into positive right away. Have faith in yourself and God.

When things go wrong, giggle and let go of the anger.

You have to have a meditated mind to wait and see what will come to you.

Through God our mind will direct us to work in the right channels and be the right channels and be in the right place at the right time and deliver.

Souls what are our souls have come here to do. We will then experience love, joy and happiness.

Our spiritual discipline has much to do with how we relate to ourselves and to each other to understand God in the Aquarian time. How we will accept ourselves and others in a state of grace without needing to control or change the situation? And the effect it will have on our social world?

Believe in that which is not, in order that it may be the imagination is the creative power in our hands. Everything in which we have faith to succeed.

For 3,000 years, man has been told to find a Guru. For the Age of Aquarius, without Guru there is no darkness.

The embodiment of the body of the word of God is the Shabad Guru, and that was something which was explained in a simple language of Guru is, you do not have to find it. "Guru is"

Where the Guru is there shall be no darkness. The impact by the words will vibrate exactly to the orientation, permutation and combination of that micro-consciousness and psyche which is, and shall always be. There shall be no duality, no disconnecting of the self to go through the cycle of change into finding and questioning one self *landing* in a lot of tragedies.

Meditation

Drop the fear and learn to hear

Meditation works in the interlock of your head and heart that blocks your ability to actually listen to another person.

Communicate for a better tomorrow, not to spoil today.

Saying one wrong word can do much more wrong than you could ever imagine, even estimate.

Engulf the situation by bringing a smile to it.

Communication

With the Age of Aquarian we should not fight about how we should worship God, since there is One God who breathes in all of us. You should clean your bodies and your minds, go out and earn a living, righteously, and share with others who are less fortunate.

The human race is about to go berserk. If you are looking for peace, YOU ARE THE PEACE. You create the peace. You are part of the peace. When good comes we should share it. When bad comes we expel it.

Three things in life—peace of mind, peace of a nation and peace of the world. If the mind is not at peace it does not have harmony. It cannot win the war of challenge. A person may look beautiful; buy the whole world with money but that person shall be unfulfilled, empty and unhappy.

Many people have taken up yoga to help relieve stress, cope with anger and build self-esteem.

Soon we will actually enter the Aquarian Age. We have seen the world through the turmoil and it is not over yet. Drastic changes are happening everywhere. "Nothing can remain hidden." As the new age enters, a lot more is bound to surface.

"INFINITY has everything. When you relate to Infinity, "Infinity gives you everything."

When you give up a lot of things, we give for the sake of giving. We give for the sake of a better relationship. It is second nature to give. Maybe we have not learned to give unconditionally. The only person who can give unconditionally is one who feels that comes from God.

To quit is to let go, to let go is to open up; to open up is to receive.

When you pray for your children and see things wrong, don't give them any energy.

When you face tragedy you should apply spiritual strength. It takes one thought to make an enemy and a friend. One Guru said the animosity against the United States is that America was under attack. (This is the first time in the world civilians have been attacked in this way.)

"It took just a handful of people to put their life at stake can do all this. The Guru said it is true we have a collective responsibility.

We are one. We will also suffer as one, and we'll act as one. All these people who died had not even a thought this only thought. Their only crime was that they were Americans. Understand it was a well-planned attack.

You figure it out that when I'm crying that the Age of Aquarius is coming, this is a period of insanity beforehand. Do you believe it? See what has happened, and now more things are expected. It is a tragedy we have to face. Tomorrow when they count everything it will be a bigger tragedy than it is today.

We offer our prayers—in silence, our heads bowed to the Almighty seeking His protection, compassion for those left behind, healing energy for those who are injured. Pray from our hearts to God Almighty.

It shows we are always open to danger. As in World War II, Japan attacked Pearl Harbor, we could have pocketed it, but we didn't.

Guru said It's the faculty of every American to keep on pocketing a lot of things until it goes over the line. Then we won't pocket it anymore. That is the way America will go. Pearl Harbor brought World War II and made us participate. Our whole lifestyle changed. We were no the same again and we are not going to be the same again.

This is what religion is all about. Search your inside, give yourself a chance, eliminate your fantasies and your imaginations. Don't live in a dream world. Things can happen and that is what has happened. The enemies plan all the time. You have to defend a thousand times;

the enemy wants one chance, which they got when the World Trade Center was attacked.

Now it is upon the nation to respond. If America does not respond, these kinds of things will be repeated.

Now is the time to reaction. The concept, which was given to saints and soldiers, comes in handy. We have to be a soldier for the insanity and a saint for this kind of insanity. You have to defend yourself in a saintly, firm way.

We have to have spiritual strength, "applied spiritual strength." Time is on us. We have to relate both to our inner and outer strength.

"America will act with one voice, with one determination and with one strength which is huge."

"We owe our thoughts to the land we live in."

In these Tumultuous times Always check with your health practitioner before making any changes to your dietary and exercise programs.

A lot of water, fresh juice, if possible, cucumbers and celery for the nervous system, watermelon to cool the liver. If you are angry, carrot is a great anti-oxidant. Focus eating on more greens, fresh fruits and vegetables, and whole grains. Avoid processed foods and refined sugar.

Supplements: a good multi vitamin, vitamin A, C, E and selenium, an essential fatty acid, a good B vitamin, when the body is stressed. Healing acupuncture, chiropractic, and massage to keep the energy flowing smoothly. Long deep breathing can calm and relax the body. Left nostril breathing can calm and soon the mind. Yoga can strengthen the nervous system to give you energy and strength. Meditation to help subconscious mind process life's events to heal others and to relax.

"Did you know that there are 108 elements in this Universe which are at the tip of your fingers, provided you decide to be compassionate, kind and caring." But as you expand in kindness, prosperity comes with it.

No matter whom we write about we are one and soon will be together. That is why we are here. We are supposed to serve, help, liberate, share with others and God will share with you.

All we need is to forget who we are and help another person. Reach out; this is the life. We are on this planet to serve people.

Have your heard yourself say, "I have no time to spare," "In time to come . . ." and "In the past?" These thoughts are what keep us from experiencing the moment. There is nothing more important than bringing your full attention into what you are doing **right now**.

We have to watch our thoughts by learning to control our thoughts. We enable ourselves to control our lives. Having freedom in our thoughts frees us in every facet of our lives. Our thoughts become feelings, our feelings become our emotions. Then our emotions become our desires and desires overtake you to the point of utter misery if you don't reach your desired goals or objects.

Different meditations help you to succeed in anything you want to be. After all, it is just a thought!

A mantra is like a telephone. God is like a telephone. There are a lot of lines in God's houses. If he doesn't answer, leave a message. Call on God—the entire world will call on you.

The ideal that a disciplined spiritual practice brings health, humility and wisdom.

The Aquarian Times will show us a whole new view of prosperity.

Fear, You have not seen the light inspire each other. We are all together in the consciousness of the one creator.

Impress the whole world can serve everyone. Will have the whole world in the palm of your hand.

No limit I what you can do.

Forget the past. Walk in the light.

CHAPTER 2

Transformation Awaken

Transformation Awaken to your destiny—connect with your soul to connect with the Infinite. Fall in love with the experience of your soul

"Singing is So Good For the Soul."

With yoga, meditation, and chanting, all these can lift you from depression, insecurity, nightmares and loss. Imparts patience and stability, self esteem—into complete self-confidence, into complete self-confidence. When you feel a sense of failure within the self, grants grace will show you the way to find your path in life, brings freedom and liberation, gives knowledge, brings freedom. With meditation, changing inner silence helps to remove the veil of illusion.

The technology of yoga and the secrets of the body.

If you listen pain and sin are erased.

Dine deep into the ocean of virtue.

Only one who has faith comes to know such a state of mind.

The faithful know all about all worlds and realms.

The path of the faithful shall never be blocked. The faithful shall depart with honor and fame.

When your body and feet (?) all deity you can wash it away. But when the intellect is polluted by sin, actions repeated over and over are engraved on the soul. You shall harvest what you plant.

Let your spiritual wisdom be your food and compassion your attendant.

Having created the creation, the Creator Lord watches over it.

Remember by the deeds and their actions they shall be judged.

The good and the bad shall be judged.

CHAPTER 3

Reflections

Evil is what uses a person. They are victims of evil. You give evil the power to hurt you.

What you see in others is a reflection of you!

There are no limitations to the imagination.

Don't change the world, change yourself.

Snap out of the way you feel.

You should have a strong determination to succeed.

We will pass this way only once so if you can do good for anyone, do it now.

Call on your loved ones in the spirit world. They are waiting to hear from you. They are just beyond the physical world.

Arise. Awake your own inner self. Lighten up, don't worry. Drink a cup of joy.

When you love your enemies, God will surely come Looking for you.

God holds the key to the mystery of life and death.

Have authority over your illness.

The truth makes all things possible.

Invite God's will to become your will.

Why worry, why fear? The Lord of the Universe is watching over you.

Knowledge is the true giver of light.

We must trust God's will to become our will.

Relax. Let the tension in you flow like water.

Bow to our heart and thank it.

Love people for who they are, not what they are.

Your body is a temple and it goes with us always.

Because the power of illusion we are not able to experience our true self. Let go of the lower self through mediation and selfless service.

Know God to know the truth, to experience love unconditionally.

When we become quiet in every sense of word. We get rid of things we do not need to have. The self will shine forth.

When you are silent and at peace, actions happen for you and for the benefit of the world.

Always worship the Self. Until that there is worship of the self. It does not matter how many churches we visit, temples, there is no real peace, But when we worship the self, then we attain true happiness and our contentment.

A spiritual path is not just a set of riches if it is done with nothing but love.

The Self is everywhere and in every thing. You don't have to give up things because you can find God right where he is.

Take a broom and sweep your heart clean.

Give up your ego. It is the self that perceives through the senses.

Worship Y our Own Self. Pursue this awareness. I am the Self. Keep worshiping your own self cause God dwells within you as you,

Poor indeed is he who does not ever show anger but worse indeed is he who cannot control it in himself. And they must fail. Though often those who flare up quickly, also forgive quickly if they remain as little children asking, seeking, living "Guide thou me, O God in the steps I take and in the words I say day by day."

God exists in all people, he is present in every heart. And you don't have to do something else to look for him.

Doubt is your worst enemy. "When you give up your doubts, knowledge spontaneously arises from within." Have faith.

Whatever you practice, that is what becomes you.

"Inner wealth comes from within, then your world will turn into nectar."

Only through the power of faith you become free everywhere in this world. No more obstacles will be in your way.

Put aside gossip. Chant God's name.

By using your energy, inhale this energy. He is right within you . . . lives in you and in your heart. This is the true house of God.

"There is no place or no person where God does not exist."

Once you know what is good for you or what is harmful, you must Choose for yourself what is beneficial.

When we celebrate a great being, that greatness manifest in your own being. Let your greatness be expressed toward others.

Know the truth and the truth will set you free.

Whatever related to yesterday is only a memory. Energy you used talking about yesterday will take away the energy you need to handle tomorrow.

We have the freedom to choose the experience of bondage of worldly life experience the truth of our perfection.

Just Look in the mirror of your heart. You will know what you are.

Give yourself some time everyday; it will take away the rough edges. It will take away the soon from the light that you are. That light will reveal itself trough you,

CHAPTER 4

The Self

The vibrations of the whole world pass through your body. Because there is a constant exchange between you and your surroundings and the people who come in contact. But to receive another magnetism, you must be near him.

Hypnotism has been called animal magnetism; it's a sort of mental chloroform through the suggestions of the hypnotist. Spiritual magnetism is something else. It is the power of the soul to attract or create whatever needs for happiness and well being.

Sometimes I think the body is like a computer. It's how you use it.

We are all connected in some way, and we will all meet again.

Fasting cleanses your blood, gives rest to the organs, revitalized energy through your lips and hands and feet. You can transmit healing energy to others when praying.

When you are weak you will receive others' vibrations.

Shun the company of those with bad habits; only the strong-minded can mingle with such people without being affected themselves.

Man's life is cut of years of his life with the noisy vibrations and noise. Vibrations of all kinds affect the nervous system. If you become calm and strong in your mind it cannot touch you.

Think, "I am happy" every day. Affirm that thought. You will develop your own magnetism to change yourself for the better. Always keep your body, clothes clean and neat.

Mix only with people you want to be. You can steal magnetism from Saints, other people thousands of miles away. Their spiritual vibrations are limitless.

Offer hour prayers in silence with our heads bowed to the Almighty seeking His protection, kindness and compassion for those left behind, seeking the healing energy for those who are injured. Let us pray from our heads to God Almighty.

If a person speaks with only his soul, people will want to listen. You can change others with just your words. This is magnetism.

Everything is a state of mind. You can make yourself happy or unhappy.

You can feel that a person is leaving this world. My mom and I were at the club I go to. We were sitting and watching people dance. After the dance this couple was leaving the floor and I told my mom that man is going to die shortly. He did two weeks later. I heard he was in his garden and did not feel well. He went into his house, laid on the bed and two hours later died. It is just at times I'm really in tune with the universe. When I go shopping, I glance at those books on the way out and I said something is only to happen to that movie star—two weeks later I found they broke up.

It is said to see the prejudice in the hearts of people in all the Religions today, but be loyal to your own. All various paths lead to God.

Through this control you will attain self-mastery and real happiness.

Your thoughts can uplift you or degrade you.

You are the master of moments of your life. Use this wisely. Always have right thoughts, don't sit with people and play cards in a smoke-filled room. It will be a waste of life and the most vicious thing you can do for your soul. It is better you take a walk, and a nap and get some healthful exercise.

The words that come out of the cannon of the mouth have the power to explode empires.

You should do something good every day instead of useless things. Each day do something worthwhile. This will make your life more meaningful.

Watch your thoughts and all your experiences because they can percolate through your thoughts.

Be careful who your friends are. They reflect you and you reflect them.

You have to control your senses or they will control you.

I'm sure many people felt this vibration but did not know how to act on it.

One night I was meditating on my friend's son whom I did not hear from for about four years. When I got done meditating, within seconds the phone rang and it was him.

It is not fair, to expect or demand the ultimate perfection from another human being. We ourselves are not perfect. "We should not expect nothing from others, but much of ourselves." Like a marriage two people have that attitude expecting nothing from the other, but much of themselves. Marriage should be based on giving. It is sad to see the way marriage is today. I once read that forty thousand couples, husband and wife, talked to each other on an average of 27 minutes a week.

Talk to each other—don't assume that your spouse can guess what is on your mind. This is why God gave us a mouth. Don't take for granted that your husband your wife knows of your love. Express that affection.

Wisdom and prayer. When people pray their minds are on food and going out or other stray thoughts. If you keep on praying in spite of mental wandering those thoughts will eventually settle down. You should feel God in your life, or you will never be happy. What your soul has lost from the time of Adam and Eve is the joy that is God.

Talent is nothing but one hundred percent attention applied in some previous life, that is what genius is.

Communion with God in daily meditation and prayer are our greatest weapons against disease, sorrow, misunderstanding, and other forms of in harmony. Keep God's presence within you always.

The kind of food you eat has a great effect on your development of a good or bad disposition. Let your food be your medicine; let your medicine be your food.

If you give up things you will have more freedom and power than ever before.

If you become in tuned with God. If God is for you, who can be against you?

Harmony is the fact, this world is only a dream.

Use your divine mind.

Use mind is the source of all movement.

Power of thought can meet your needs anywhere.

Some people have no control over themselves, it is a lack of weakness.

It is God's love that loves man, not man's God.

Turn you past and future over to God.

When you search for love, I will always love you.

Don't wait for someone to hug you, hug yourself three times a day.

Anything that is related to yesterday is only a memory; don't waste your energy on yesterday it will take away the energy you need to handle tomorrow.

Food is only ordinary matter but it carries the feelings of the person who made it and served it.

Don't waste time on other's mistakes.

Don't use God as an excuse for your mistakes.

Know your path in life is free; just don't separate yourself from God.

Fill all your channels with truth and love.

You are the loved of love.

With the power of thought you can heal anyone thousands of miles away.

Human pity causes pain and suffering.

Angel thoughts are God's thoughts passing to man.

Don't be conformed to this world, but transformed.

Have only light thoughts.

Clear the mind.

Believe all things are possible. Great fears will disappear.

Love people for who they are, not what they are.

Let everything unfolded like a flower and see the beauty in your life.

If anything happens to you, just say I am better from this mistake.

Remember it isn't what you eat, it is what you eat mentally.

Take charge of your life and your thoughts and you can do anything.

We have eyes and ears, but sometimes we don't see and sometimes we don't hear.

Don't lower yourself to anyone else's level.

Healing is a lack of love and forgiveness.

Don't talk about something so it does not materialize.

Don't waste your energy on others. You are not accountable for other's actions.

Don't wait for someone to love you, love yourself.

Repeat love when a negative thought comes up.

Every lie is a lack of faith.

You create your destiny.

Time is the absolute merge into the absolute.

Peace and love. Pour in peace and love.

You are a reflection of what you see spiritually.

Reflection, look in the mirror you act supreme.

Failure is a stepping-stone toward future success.

Don't have faith in matter.

Don't look at the things that are seen, but unseen. But the things seen are temporal, but the things that are unseen are eternal.

Dismiss your illness.

The sooner you dump unhealthy thoughts, the faster healing can come!!!

Stay on a spiritual path, "know the self." Tap into your infinite source of energy and psyche.

Forgive yourself. Have guts to get rid of pain and fear.

Have faith in yourself and you can do anything.

Don't be enslaved, don't be a prisoner in your own body.

If you are looking for a mate there is a right time, a right place, a right person, what blesses one blesses all.

Listen rather than talk.

Watch your thoughts they become your words. Watch your words, they become your actions. Watch your actions, they become your habits. Watch your habits, they become your character. Watch your character, it becomes your life.

At the end of the day ask your angels to guide you

Always remain in control and calm let the universe come in and let everything else go.

This is the present, the past is dead and the future will take care of itself,'

Don't be afraid to ask God.

If you want perfection, win the grace of your mind. Keep it calm and serene.

If you want freedom, if you want perfection, win the grace of your mind.

You have enough grace in your heart to fill this entire universe.

Don't wait for someone to thank you. Thank yourself.

If you are with someone and you break up, remember together you expressed God's goodness and likeness and now it is gone. It came from God and is still with you both. It came from your consciousness but you felt was your own completeness it doesn't take another person to make your life that way. You are complete.

A person should be in a position to hold his values clearly in his consciousness.

The price of God is living without doubt. So don't doubt, trust God.

Get rid of your ego so nothing can destroy you.

When you meditate empty yourself and let the universe come into you.

The secret of the soul is awareness.

There is so much tension in life that we miss opportunities that come our way.

Your intuition can be your best friend. When you're in trouble, close your eyes and think. That will be the best thing to do.

The purpose in life is to do something that will live forever.

In the Age of Aquarius, if you don't have the technical knowledge of the self, it will destroy you.

If you speak wrong words it will haunt you until your death.

As you think, so you are.

Everyone has a mission to fulfill. If you do it with devotion and conviction, success comes from all sides.

Everyone is precious. Even the most rotten person was made by God.

For every loss there is a gain. For every gain there is a loss.

If you are insecure, bad things will happen. If you don't feel insecure, they will go away.

Experience yourself and everything inside you so you won't be a victim of your own permanent fear.

Our life is very sacred.

Everything is within you; attitude, gratitude and happiness will come to you and go where you go.

There is nothing in life more worthy, more beautiful than you,

We live by the breath. We were born by the breath and when you die the breath leaves you.

Communication, speak through music.

No one should control anyone. You should flow together like a river and end up in the same ocean.

Live wise and Divinely so we don't have to live in any duality.

People imprison themselves to sex, food and their way of life. Some people are more afraid of the truth than of life.

Never try to solve a fear—drop a fear. Take it to the highest part of you and drop them.

When you smile, you will have people in the palm of your hand.

If you love great you become great. If you love small things, you become small/

Life is a flow of love.

Wisdom is telling the truth.

When you have pain or fear, you have to forgive yourself.

We should be a lighthouse to serve people and lift them.

Meditation can calm the mind and develop your intuition so you can recognize what is real and important to you.

The injury of the tongue is far deeper than the cut of the sword.

We meditate to keep our minds sharp and alert. Canting mantras to our souls so we can walk in the light.

When you have a problem meditate and face it.

The problem in this world is stress.

Make your mind a servant, not a master.

The best theory is record your voice, and then listen to it.

When you bless everyone then you will be blessed.

When you eat or where you eat has a direct and indirect influence on your mind, body and spiritual awareness.

Your physical body is a temple; take care of it.

If you're not spiritually strong we can't negotiate properly. If you are not mentally strong, we don't have the grit to negotiate. Then we build more guns and bombs.

Bring out your inner best. That is the secret of success.

Some people born out of an inferior complex.

Keep your body strong so you can do anything,.

The imagination is the creative power in our hands.

No matter how things go always keep cool.

With the Age of Aquarius it will be a new time. You should purify your mind, body and soul. This age will serve us of our awareness and experience.

Believe all things are possible. It is your strength, pride and should. If you don't want to deal with it, then call it impossible. If it is impossible for god, it's possible for man.

Yoga is a science. It is the purest act by which to life.

If you don't discipline yourself you will never know who you are.

When the Muslims conquered India, they destroyed the literature of yoga. They feared the capacity of yoga to make people unconquerable.

Talk you your problems

The thing we can do is restore peace in this turbulent times have peace within ourselves.

What ever happens be grateful and hopeful.

Take time throughout the day—take a minute to be yourself, love yourself, feel divine. Take a minute to be yourself. Feel peace within yourself and with everybody.

If we stop judging ourselves and others we would be living in paradise.

You should take control of your life so you can deal with everything with love and kindness.

Knowledge is not outside, it comes from within you. If you direct it, it will become the knower of all. So if you direct it otherwise you will become very miserable off.

If anyone slanders you or depresses you give it to God.

When you speak from the heart you can rule. But when you speak from the heart you destroy.

Don't limit your fear, then you will have unlimited power of inspiration.

Always keep the faith.

Whatever we say lives forever. But a wrong word can change your image.

Always know you are part of the universe and the universe is part of you.

If you cannot elevate others then you have no power.

Life is a balance to give you the experience to let you discover the you within you. Remember we are always being tested. You must find your own depth and test it.

You are a "hu-man being." "Hu" means spirit, the light. "Man" means the mental. You are the spirit of your mind. And the bright light of yourself.

Some people think being religious is about what you believe. Your spirit is the hub. I am one I am. Don't factor your dignity or personality. Then you achieve that, all wealth comes to you.

Bless yourself. Honor your grace that God will guide us and give us strength to serve and bring peace.

You can be a slave to your way of life.

Some people are afraid of the truth than life. We confine ourselves.

No one can put you in prison except yourself.

Happiness and Honesty comes from honest living.

We are all born to relate to the future; to silence that will speak to you. And the radiance that will give you absolute selflessness.

If you make yourself happy when people look at you they will be happy too.

Being old you need wisdom and grace. You will always be rich if you are wise.

A lie is a loss of face.

We forget who we are but we are one with God and we should inspire others.

Your personality has no power but your performance has power.

When you bless your enemies and reach out to love the source and cause of calamity, God will be with you.

If you get depressed woman take a cold shower, massage yourself with a towel. Start with the feet until your body turns red. Your thoughts will go away.

Isolation is your own fear.

We are on a journey going through a planetary shift.

A coin has two sides if you get angry, or mad, or emotional, turn it over and look at the other side.

When people are obnoxious they can't change; their behavior is self damaging.

Spirituality is not a religion, it is facing yourself with a smile when life confronts you.

Remember yourself. God rotates this earth; God will take care of your routine.

There are no blocks in this world. The only blocks are you.

People suffer because of impure food and impure thoughts and deeds.

Life and let live. Just keep on going.

If you don't get anywhere in life it is because you limit yourself.

You are the master of your destiny.

The Age of Aquarius is upon us. It is the age of peace, tranquility, dignity, grace and sharing. Soon we will all be united.

May God bless all of us and all creatures.

Just follow the path of wisdom of your mind.

When all rivers come together as one—in the Aquarian Age, we will come together to become one.

When you act like God then everything will come to you.

Start to meditate and clear your mind so you can face the challenges and pressure.

When you follow the grace of your mind, you will win.

We are not bound to this world. We have freedom.

CHAPTER 5

Quotes

Today is today—Because tomorrow is not

1. Temperance—Eat not to dullness, drink not to elevation
2. Silence—Speak not what may benefit others
3. Order—Let all things have their place.
4. Resolution—Resolve to perform what you ought; perform without fail what you resolve.
5. Sincerity—Use no hurtful deceit' think innocently.
6. Justice—Wrong no one by doing injuries, or omitting the benefit that you are deity.
7. Moderation—Avoid extremes, forbear resenting injuries so much as you think they deserve.

Cleanliness—Tolerate no uncleanliness in body, clothes or habitation.

Concentrate on one principle for an entire week, every day of the week. Respond by proper action every time an occasion arises. The second week let your subconscious mind take over.

He who cannot forgive destroy that bridge over which some day he may need to pass.

The man of real capabilities, the high thinker, the educated man has no time to spend digging up old skeletons from the closet.

What ever any man did in the past he himself is accountable to God. It is written down in all its naked truth in his consciousness.

If a spider catches a fly in the web and that fly is strong enough to breath that enables and escapes, he is a free fly.

Prana means energy. Breathing quiets the mind he physical, mental, and spiritual levels.

It is not what you get out of life that counts; it is what you put into life that counts.

Fear: Look in the mirror, it reflects you just like a candle reflects. Have no fear. "I'm the master of myself."

Auto Suggestion: Use your imagination, everyday in every respect. I am getting better and better. Say it twenty times in the morning and evening.

Repeat: My life is better and beautiful. If you are troubled say, "No" it does not trouble me at all, not in the least. Every idea is true and transforms itself into action.

God is with me; God is for me, so who can be against me.

By letting go it all gets done, the world is won by those who let go. But when you try and try, it is even beyond the winning.

It isn't what you get out of life that counts; it is what you put into life that counts.

As a man soweth so shall he reap, as an attitude is held towards another that is gradually built within self.

Hence the urge, as it were, to hold what would be called malice, and ever determining within the self. "I'll get even with you yet" doesn't pay, for this only builds into self that held in thought miracles.

Find less fault with others, and they will find less fault with thee.

The way you look at others reflects to small degree the way you truly view yourself in the inner levels of consciousness.

There is a lot of power through people.

Remember opportunity never stops knocking.

Each night burn the records of the day; at sunrise every soul is born again.

Look at one thing, to see another, to understand what you see is a third, but what you understand is still something else. But to act on what you learn is all that really matters.

You make people think they're thinking, they will love you. But if you really make them think they hate you!!

The way we think is the way we live.

Remember we picked this life so we have to live it out, if you don't like your life only you have to change it. Watch your thoughts the way you think is the way you live. On this there is no limit to how much we can learn, it is never to late, if we will only acquire that most important single piece of knowledge, that is the knowledge of how little we really know. God gave you a mind to use. It's never to late.

Call on your higher self.

"Our mind is our only weapon," it's the greatest leveler of all things; You have to control your thoughts so they don't control you.

To look at one thing, to see what you look at is another, to understand what you see is a third, to learn from what you understand is still something else. But to act on what you learn is all that should matter.

However things go, in life you must remain calm, quiet and peaceful. This peace is the source of prosperity. Self containment-this is the act of prosperity and it is the highest spiritual strength. Nothing can match it.

There is an ocean of life within all of us. It is the love of God. It is so pure; it is unconditional. It is always that. Just let yourself to drink this love. God is fully present within us. If you make a simple effort you can experience God. Let this understanding that take you higher and higher. Let is make you feel more and more divine, always trust yourself.

Think my trouble is going away. Just as you think you can't open your hands. You have to address yourself to the imagination, not the will. While wiping our hand over your forehead, say it is going away; it is going away 20 to 30 seconds. It should work you keep repeating it.

When you enter a home think of peace in that home, peace in yourself and think of that person being healed.

Opportunity never stops knocking.

Every night burn the records of the day. At sunrise every soul is born again.

Auto Suggestion.

Positive; you can do it. Negative; you can't do it. You will feel active, full of life-cheerful fit.

Self Mastery

Our actions spring not from our will but from imagination, the influence of the imagination upon the moral and physical being of mankind. Of course the thing must be win our power.

Every thought entirely filling our mind becomes true for us and tends to transform itself into action. Say every day in every way, I'm getting better and better.

You Are What You Think.

All that we think becomes true for us. We must not then allow ourselves to think wrongly.

Nothing in life is to be feared; it is only to be understood.

Call Death

1. You call it death, this seeming endless sleep. We call it birth. The soul at last set free.
2. It's hampered not by time or space. You weep. Why weep at death. It's immorality.

In the shower sing some kind of loud prayer, and sit or stand in any position and wear white clothes for fifteen minutes. If you're depressed, for a half an hour.

Some people are better off making mistakes than making decisions.

People who don't find time for recreation, sooner or later they will find time for illness.

"The might be's and what will happen they should not concern you now."

Actions may not always bring happiness; but there is no happiness without action.

STOP procrastinating. You will gain more weight.

It is not the place or condition but you alone can make anyone happy or miserable.

"You may have had many troubles in your life but I bet they never came."

What you do that is the only required of you, you are a slave. But the moment you do more, you are a free man.

Think of your life more as a stepping stone toward a more positive life and attitude.

Take off your blinders so you can see the world.

Boredom will make you old before your time.

Remember the person who lives by himself or for himself is apt to be corrupted by his own company he keeps.

You do a lot more by smiling instead of frowning.

Your face isn't glass. It won't crack.

Learn to laugh at life; life is too short to hold anger, fear, the past and now.

When you pray, "please" pray for the world and all those concerned. It will make you feel better as a human being instead of thinking of yourself.

You worry about everything but the outcome it may never materialize.

Like some people get indigestion before they eat.

Know your fears, don't hide your fears. Say this is my fear, get rid of it.

If you take care of the present, the future will take care of itself.'

Since man has free will, he is responsible for his actions.

Reason is useless, man should turn to faith.

Don't worry about tomorrow. You will have less time to enjoy today. We only pass through this world but once so don't open your umbrella while the sun is still shining.

If you keep your good deeds a secret, blessings and rewards will be showered upon you.

It is mind over matter when you say you can't do it, but most of the time you can. Use your subconscious mind for a few months to achieve things. Train your body.

Recharge your body with play, rest and sleep.

You will have better health having positive thoughts and attitudes.

Always have something to live for. When you have something to live for the subconscious mind forces upon the conscious mind strong motivating factors to keep you alive.

Remember that the things that are unseen; for the things that are transient, but the things that are unseen are eternal.

The price of ignorance is sin, sickness and death. Some influences may be mental figments of the imagination. Knowledge is power if only put to use.

Thinking good positive and cheerful thoughts will improve the way you feel. What affects your mind effects your body. Develop a positive mental attitude.

I Feel Healthy
I Feel Happy
I Feel Terrific

Enjoy a good life and live longer with a positive mental attitude.
Be happy. Great things are in store for you.
Have the inner urge to do something.
Remember don't take everything for granted.
Faith without works are dead.
Direct your thoughts; control your emotions and ordain your destiny.
Success is having a positive mental attitude. You will have everything to gain and nothing to lose.
Faith without words is dead.
God is for us. Who can be against us?
You should direct your thoughts; control your emotions to ordain your destiny.
Through action you get things done.
Open your heart to the universe of love and he will fill you up.
Who are we? We are the product of our life, our environment, physical body, conscious and subconscious mind, experience, and heredity.
Have always the courage to face the truth.
Satisfaction is a mental attitude.
Defeat can be a stepping-stone or a stumbling block.
If you can spend the time on doing something you won't have much time for accomplishing.
If you keep dwelling on the past and your misfortunes, the greater the power will hurt you.
The greatest mistake of all is if you do nothing.
The purpose in life is to live your life.
Success is a state of mind.
If nothing works out, let it go.

Some people go the extra mile, some have accurate thinking. You should have self-discipline, a pleasing personality, enthusiasm, creative vision, budgeting your time and money, teamwork.

Keep your mind positive. If your mind is right, your world will be right. There will never be another like you.

Change your world, and you can achieve anything worthwhile in your life; use your positive mental attitude. It can change your world.

Have hope in yourself and others.

Having confidence in children will give them confidence in themselves.

Set your goals. Write them down. Set a deadline. Set your standards high. Achieve your goals.

People are happy as they make up their minds to be. It is a state of mind of being happy or unhappy.

Living with someone their energy level and capacities may not be the same as yours. You may not think alike, but attract and repel through verbal communications. You Are What You Think.

A positive mental attitude can attract you to all the health, wealth, and happiness you desire.

If a man is right his world will be right.

If you share unhappiness and misery you will attract unhappiness and misery. Be careful who your friends are. They reflect you and you reflect them.

What you think so you are.

If you want something in life you should work for it.

If you have a guilt feeling, it's good, but get rid of it.

Awaken the sleeping giant within you.

There is a devil there is no doubt. Is he trying to get in us or trying to get out?

Be careful when you pick your friends. They reflect you and you reflect them.

Man has forgotten his God. Man thinks too much of himself.

You only have to answer to one person and that person is God.

Failure comes from within.

We are never alone. We have our loved ones in the spirit world.

Wisdom is the ability to benefit from someone else's experiences.

If someone hurts you, forgive them and in hear and your heart will be free and happy and you will continue and be able to have a better life.

Always thank God if life is good or bad.

Everything in life is possible; you will always have miracles happen to you,

Every time you lie to a friend it's another shovel of dirt on your grave.

Highest mental power of a man willing to cope with a condition that is infinitely beyond his control and he faces it with the belief that he is going to come through it.

Eating when, how, where direct influence on your mind, body and spiritual awareness.

Forgive the past. Walk in the light.

Nobody can control anybody. All you can do is flow with each other like a river and streams flow together and end up in the same ocean.

To get rid of fear, pain, you have to have the guts!! To forgive yourself. Just forgive yourself.

When the body receives healing from you, this is the best healing.

If you are depressed, moody, anger and rude, empty what is inside should be stronger than what is outside.

Don't go through life with blinders on.

Sometimes we thoroughly the mental influence on the wrong side hurting those we mean to bless.

When you give up things you will have more freedom and power and passions then we ever had before.

The past is done; the future will take care itself.

Know that life is full of limitations but it's just the opposite. There are endless opportunities. It's just a matter of listening and moving ahead.

Half of your life burdens will go away if you just forgive your earthly parents. Just remember, they are good and they did their best.

Life is just a lease on time and space. It is now that you can secure your tomorrow. It's now that you can elevate yourself. Now to learn to be grateful so your confidence in yourself and your reputation can travel before you.

Dance away stress and fears. If you're uptight, you will be dead by tonight.

Eating when, how, where, direct influence on your mind, body and spiritual awareness.

The highest mental power of man willing to cope with a condition that is infinitely beyond his control and he faces it with the belief that he is going to come through with it.

Take one minute to breath in love. One minute to feel divine and one minute to feel peace with everyone.

A person should forgive themselves first before giving advice to someone else.

People value old coins, cheese and wine. But we do not value older people. They lose their hearing. It's because no one wants to talk to them anymore. They seem to tune out the world around them.

Remember when a man of brass or iron guards the state, it will be destroyed.

Prayer is the question. Meditation is the answer.

Remember every day in every way you are getting better and better through a positive mental attitude.

No more energy is consumed in using your brain that is just keeping it alive. Don't be afraid to use it.

Think with your mind, not with your emotions.

Sometimes it is easier to believe a lie that has been heard a thousand times than to believe a fact that one has never heard before.

If you want to get rid of a problem, write it on paper and burn it.

If you ask a question you may be a fool for five minutes. But if you don't ask a question you remain a fool forever.

If you want something done, give it to a man who is busy. He'll find the time for it.

Just look ahead at least tomorrow, as we are each an entity in ourselves.

Don't be so hard on yourself. Speaking from experience, I myself have been through more than you will ever know or go through what I did. Laugh at life, know your fears, and get rid of them. What happened a few minutes ago will never happen again. Don't drag the past with within you, it is only dead weight, get rid of it and you will feel like you lost weight and you really might lose a few pounds. Your attitude will change, as well and the world in your life will get better. Don't hang on to the past. Your future is bright ahead. Always read books by people who practice what they preach.

You can conquer the world by being noble. Being noble is a virtue.

To be an angel you must have compassion and grace; don't be a social animal.

In the Age of Aquarius there will be no religion. It will be if you experience or not experience it. It will be your own spiritual efficiency that is with you.

You should know yourself and the truth about yourself.

When you have a chance to say something, speak it from your guts and your soul.

I believe we have had many previous incarnations.

When your health and wealth are gone, but when your character is gone, everything is gone.

Remember a hungry soul can corrupt your mind and body.

The way you feel don't be afraid to stand out in a crowd of people. You will become more spiritual.

Sometimes you know all without direction. But without direction you will never find your destination.

People should live their lives with compassion and love. It would be a better world.

Some people think they are somebody when they are Nobody.

If you doubt you will live in pain.

We should always be grateful for everything around us.

Be kind to yourself and you will be kind to others.

Always do everything with grace. This is your identity.

Always do everything with grace.

Always love yourself.

In life you should know who you are and what you want and where you are going.

If you want to succeed in life listen to your consciousness.

Sometimes you just have to learn to listen.

Sometimes people suffer because they didn't confront their problem.

If you don't want to be forgotten or another person just kind words they will never forget it.

Body is a temple. Take care of it.

When you feel the world is caving in on you meditate.

If we were born to be together then we should enjoy the fruits of this life.

Always tell the truth because no matter what it will come out anyway.

We should try to base everything on love.

Forgive yourself and your past so you can walk in the light.

Take time throughout the day for even just a minute to be yourself. Feel peace with the Universe.

To be in a state of tranquility at all times you can flow like water.

What ever you achieve in life is your character.

Never think you are perfect. You are.

If we forgive our parents many of our burdens will go away.

If you have or any trouble just hold your breath sixteen seconds; it will change your zone and hemispheres will change. Your body will know the difference.

If you tell people they are beautiful they don't need makeup some people have beauty on the outside, ugly on the inside.

When you start blessing others, then you will be blessed.

What ever you can do or experience in life do it with grace.

For the little time we are here we should leave behind a legacy. Always keep the faith. Never give up.

Don't be a slave in your own body. Just know we are on a journey going through a planetary shift.

Remember we were all born to love each other, not kill each other. We should be serving each other.

The act of life is to always serve people.

When you star to have greed it creates corruption.

Can you understand the "you" within you; feel your own peace and love.

Your soul is your life.

When there is stress and anger, your life can cause violence.

You are in control.

Live the life of grace.

Do not cater to your children, they will disobey and leave home.

The most sensitive part of the body is the eyebrows. Plucking them takes away the Electromagnetic field inner current balance. You will never be able to control your health problems.

We have to share our values with the next generation.

You can have a relationship with your body and soul.

If you are always negative, change your life or your life will never change.

Meditation can change your state of mind.

You should ask yourself who are you—who am I?

Don't ever take advantage of others.

Prayer is very powerful. Don't forget to pray.

You should judge yourself instead of others. That will elevate you.

If you feel you are doing something and do not feel right drop it.

With prayer we all will live in happiness, love and peace.

We should only live for each other, not against them.

Wherever you go be the light. Be a lighthouse for others.

Think more of God.

Prayer is so powerful; there is nothing greater than prayer.

CHAPTER 6

Death and Dying

Everything in life is a gift from God, and life is the greatest gift of all. Some day we will have to give it back. I feel we are all connected in some way. What you see in others is a reflection of yourself. Don't look at faults in others; look at your own.

It is our destiny and we have control over it. Every action produces a reaction. We reap the consequences of our own actions. All our actions—mental, verbal, and physical—bear fruit. Whatever you sow will harvest.

If you want to solve a fear, drop it and your problems. Take it to the highest part of you and drop them.

Death is universal and predictable of human existence. We must confront death of our family, friend. But the timing of death is the most certain thing in our lives, and is uncertain. We never know when it will come. Death to some people is the indication of human failure. Technology today and wizardly regards death as something to be conquered, or delayed at any cost. The old are dying in hospitals, nursing homes with tubes, dialysis machines for a person on a machine, artificially maintained is bizarre. With drugs that dull pain, inhibit awareness of the process of dying. You should confront death entirely unprepared. The mental health profession offered me no psychological help to the dying. In the last decade result of the dying research now revived interest in death and dying among professionals and lay people. You should show respect of people who are dying. In spite of all the work that has been done, we have not developed ways to relieve the suffering of those who are dying. In traditions, an experienced knowledge of death is an integral part of the wisdom of life. With rites of passage, ancient death-rebirth mysteries, spiritual practices of other great religions. All of these traditions share the belief that when we fully accept the mortality of that aspect of ourselves—which is the ego identifies—we discover that our true identity is eternal and divine.

One of the best masters of the oldest most honored spiritual lineage of the east has an entirely difference approach, one that is relevant for those leaving us or for those facing imminent death. According to his teaching, suffering, whatever in life or death is based on the ignorance of our own real nature and on a false sense of identity. We are filled with fear but once you realize that our identity lies not in the ego or in the body, but in the subtle consciousness that operates through and beyond both our physical demise no longer represents to us the end of everything. When you get to know your real self the fear of death disappears but the suffering of life vanishes as well.

When you know the Self, both life and death will, can become enjoyable games. One Swami describes life-death cycles in terms of the doctrine or Karma, the ancient and immutable law of cause and affect. Which decrees that one must experience the consequences of every action one performs. Birth and dying are part of an endless cycle when we discover the totally free consciousness that exists within us. If we would only liberate ourselves, that energy called Adrenaline in the ancient Indian texts is recognized in virtually every spiritual tradition as the creative force of Energy of the human organism. In a human being eternal form it carries on all the functions of the organism in its internal form, it gives rise to the spiritual process. In some people it lays dormant at the base of the spine. When awakened it works on the physical and subtle level, burning physical, emotional and mental impurities and ultimately opening the individual to the experience of his or her innate nature. It can open and free us from the most rooted fears, and open us to undreamed of freedom and joy.

When God reveals Himself, within the heart this human being is great; a human being is the highest.

If a person does not know his own inner Consciousness, then his life is wasted, it is your duty to find out who you are. Look at your life and everything else you have? Are you watching it so it doesn't wither away?

When the body is burned it goes up in flames. So why do you think so much about your body? Your mind? Your wealth? Then fear is the last moment and we are afraid to leave it all behind.

We fear death for no good reason. You have to have courage and be brave in the face of death.

Death is nothing more than a long sleep. In the sleep of death one does not wake up—at least not in the same body.

When a person dies, he or she might see a light or Blue Pearl. This light enters the body when the rhythm of breathing begins. It departs from the body leaving everything limp and lifeless. The blue pearl is at the crown of the head. Some people see it when their loved ones die.

But if a person has committed bad actions, his soul will leave through the anus. According to the scripture, it is a sign that this person will go to Hell. If the should leaves through a person's eyes this means he has been very virtuous.

Death is one thing in this world that is always on time. When you committed many sins, there is nothing that can be done.

When we leave this world we take nothing with us. Our worldly life exists here has no value after we leave our bodies. But Divine wealth is our love, our compassion for others, our devotion to God. We will attain happiness and pace in this world, and when we leave it will go with us. Divine wealth buys God. Worldly wealth buys only death.

We reap the consequences of our own actions. This is God's law.

We take birth according to our actions. What we did in a past life Trough meditation, some people see their past lives and for some this is the proof of reincarnation like you have seen before in meditation.

We are born, die, born and die again and again. We transmigrate through different forms, high and low. We exhaust our Karma of he past, we create new Karma for the future. To free yourself by going within and, through meditation, discovering your own inner Self. Then we are liberated from death, you discard the ego and merge with the Self. The ego is the veil which hides the Self, and helps us bound to the body. The ego is nothing but our sense of limited individuality; our identification with the body and mind.

The purpose of life is to become free of all impurities and perform good actions, and not bad actions—or we will hurt others and ourselves. Once we become full, we are nothing but Supreme Consciousness.

In every human being is a great divine energy called *Klendaline*, that created the entire universe in total freedom. I am the Self. When you realize that God dwells within you ones own inner Self.

There is something beyond this physical body. Not just "to say this is my body. I am like this body is like saying, I am this towel, or hat." When we say this is my body we demonstrate that we are different from the body.

The waking and dream states, the witness of our thoughts and feelings is nothing but pure consciousness. The absolute Brahman (Brahman means God). This is what you discover in medication.

When you meditate you move beyond the waking dream, and sleep states to that transcendental state.

One's condition at the time of death is the result of one's actions. One should understand the value of time. With this understanding, meditate and repeat God's name. You can attain everything in this world but once time has passed you cannot get it back. We have made the journey through many lifetimes. But we must remember One is God, and the other is our own death.

Wake up before death comes to surprise you. At the time of death remember God, to remember him long before your time. If you meditate and pray every day you should have no fear of death. Some people forget the reason we came into this world, desires increased and consumed your life. You forgot Who am I, "the goal of your life? What did you accomplish here?" To indulge in sense pleasures, eat and drink and forget one day you will leave this body. The inner Self is ageless and unchanging. The Supreme truth lies within you; that the light is Self. May your awareness turn inward, live with knowledge, know you are the Supreme Truth. When you talk about death I think of my daughter when she died. It was on a Friday evening. I was at a friend's house after dinner I was wrapping the garbage and my thumb started to bleed but I did not *cut* it. I looked at the clock. It bled from 6:20 p.m. to 6:50 p.m. All I said. God I did nothing wrong but I don't feel right. That weekend I knew something happened. On Monday I got a call my daughter was dead.

My daughter was separated from her husband and I couldn't get any information from the police. I called the clinic and told them she died at 6:20 to 6:50 p.m. I thought he passed out. No sound. All he said is call the police. I went to the services. When I walked in her husband saw me and let out a big scream. My daughter and I looked alike. I found that her girlfriends found her in her hat tub on Monday morning. They called her husband and I guess he said call the police. But she was on some strong medication for her rotator cuff. But her mother-in-law told me she wanted the house key back and so she called the police to go to his work place to get it. They brought it back at 3:15 p.m. But her husband came to her house after work and he was real mad. It was a few days later I was leaving the house around 7:15 a.m. and when I came outside the sun was shining. I looked up at the sun and it just got brighter and brighter, and I could feel her presence going toward the light.

A few months after the death I had a dream this man picked up my daughter up off he couch and she was naked. He carried her down a hallway and that was the end of the dream. But the medication she was on was very powerful and she said she passed out a lot from it. They found her in her whirlpool, but she did not like hot water.

For my husband after taking care of him for ten years he went to a nursing home for a week. But three days before his life energy ran out, I was holding his hand and I started levitating and taking him to the other side. All I could think of was he has to go, not me.

I got a call from the nursing home at 11:00 clock. They had to take him to the hospital. Then the hospital called at 2 a.m. and said he was doing ok. I said I would come to the hospital. They said wait till morning, but I was with him all these years and this was the first time he was without me. I fell into a deep sleep. The phone rang at 7 a.m. I knew it was the hospital and he left this earth planet. His life energy ran out. My sister went with me and she sat in a chair crying and I was so amazed when looked at him, he looked like an angel with this aura and light around his face. I knew his mother came to take him home. I think an hour went by and all I kept saying to my sister "look at him. He looks like an angel." I did not touch him because my friend said if someone comes to you from the spirit world they have a lot of energy and could give you a heart attack. His mother came to him twice in the hospital. First she wanted him to go with her and he said no. She came back and said I say a rosary for you. He told his mother he was not ready. My husband was older than me and never believed in the spirit world and how close we are.

I dreamt we were in a hospital—priests and nuns and everything that was going on. But I saw this hallway and this number on a door and knew if my husband was in that one wing, he would die. The doctor who did the surgery said that was the worst case he ever did. A week went by and they said they were going to move him to the wing I saw in my dream. So I went down to the chapel and prayed for three hours. When I went back to see the nurse, she said something came up. We cannot move him.

At my husband's funeral, his family was there. But after we were all going to a restaurant, when we got there my sister said, "Frank's family is not coming." I stood like a stone statue from my waist down and felt like an anchor from my waist up. I was levitating for a few moments. I told my sister I feel great after ten years of putting up with his family and the daughter who wanted to control her father.

Before my dad died and we were talking, he put his hand on my face and I saw and felt this flash of light come through his hand. It as so beautiful that he gave me something before he left.

My sister and I took care of this one lady. One week she would go and I the next. I remember I was upstairs in the bedroom and I just stood real still and all I said, God forgive her for what she did and I knew she was never coming back here. This was on a Wednesday. I got a call telling me on Friday she had a seizure and to come to the hospital. I said no, you will be negative so I prayed for her. I never prayed that hard for anyone else. She had a brain tumor and died a year later. Before she passed her daughter was reading her mother's card to her. She opened her eyes of blue, took two breaths and left.

My mom and I were close before she passed on. She was so cute and said I want to try it out first—leave and come back. She was not ready to leave; she was never sick and small like me. One day she said Uncle Joe came and sat with me, but he left. But he will come back. For days she mumbled works from time to time for a day and a half like she was deleting her past from the time she was born to that time she said was at now.

I knew the night before she would be leaving before morning I could feel it. When the nurse came into the room to tell me my mom took her last breath, I stood up and this energy came over me and looked at the bottom of my foot and the wart I had for three years left. I was hanging on because I always wanted the best for my mom. I did have three doctors who could not get rid of it and I told the last doctor it will go away when I let go.

I do feel we are all connected in some way and know when something is going to happen.

My aunt ran and started Camp Will O Way for twenty-five years for the handicapped because her daughter was handicapped. So I volunteered at the camp at thirteen years old. When she passed away at sixty-one we went to the funeral. I saw a girl the same age as my cousin who was handicapped and she was touching the coffin and looked into her eyes and I said to her mother your daughter is an old soul. She said she has had one thousand past lives. And we go to the ARE Clinic by Edgar Cayce. She said my daughter is a healer.

CHAPTER 7

Wisdom

It is good every day to have a little Wisdom in your life. I feel we are one with everything that all happiness and Honesty are in us that we can never make a mistake.

We must understand our consciousness for what we want to achieve in life.

When we live and work with others we should be more coherent with the ones we work with. We should try to understand the mind of that person.

When we have forgiveness in our hearts and compassion, you will experience God within you.

Having faith in any institution you dwell in faith and reason, and happiness and radiance will fill that person.

We can be healthy, happy and holy so we can smile and shine like the sun to all human beings and have them in the palm of your hands.

Wearing white clothes is good therapy. My friend told me it is the color therapy and we to be conscious. After a bath it is good to wear white for fifteen minutes.

We should discipline ourselves in life, financially, spiritually and physically.

If you don't spend more time on yourself and your body needs, feelings you could be in trouble. Nothing will work.

Prayer is like falling in love with the infinite.

Try not to challenge phenomena in your life. The outcome could cause pain, disease misery.

I feel every human is God in himself to have compassion and merge with God.

I pray that every day peace and joy prevail for all and experience God's grace.

I believe that you can make the impossible possible. But it sometimes requires commitment and character and projection. Look ahead and see it magnetize it in you.

If you have a problem, chisel it away and you will get an answer.

Changing your food, chew your food well and mix it with saliva. You will be more healthy! Your brain will be sharper.

Love is a force to experience your higher consciousness for loving yourself, your inner being, to master the highest stage of love within you.

When you meditate you can gain a lot more achievements can be manifold.

Think well of yourself and others.

It is sometimes to avoid pressure in your every day life—if being single, married, death, and a job—choosing right from wrong. It is the way you want to go and for children the most serious part is your direction choosing right from wrong.

Doing a lot of selfless serviced is a test of selflessness and putting your life on the path of righteousness.

When you seek to someone with grace, that grace will come back to you.

In life, you should be wise essential: how you protect the self. If not you always live in self-conflict.

Having faith is very powerful institutions. When you dwell in logic, faith and reason the argument leaves and happiness and radiance will fill that person.

In all that you do show the spirit of God of being right and flow of nature. If you can do that it is a meditation.

Always ask for strength courage so you can elevate yourself to be healthy, happy and holy, and blessed with our lives and be as this spirit shining for all human beings.

Sing songs. It is a beautiful emotional release. You will be so grateful to yourself. It is a way to stay sane, another way to confront insanity. Music is good for the soul.

Be careful what you do in life because it take's forty days to get a reputation, then twenty-five years to get rid of it.

If you commit yourself and life that life as a commitment, you will find absolute infinite freedom

I pray that God will bless us with his grace and give us knowledge, wisdom to have light and remove darkness, to have compassion, to control our passion, to serve everyone with grace and love, to speak the truth at all times so we can all live in peace.

Love is so powerful when you have that love you can move mountains, it is so powerful love can never be forgotten.

No one can change your character when you are an honest person.

Never make any changes just know God is beautiful, bountiful and wonderful and he created you.

When you commit yourself to serve in any way, do it do it with love, kindness, and affection. It will satisfy you and give you trust.

Life is a gift, it is essential energy, it is a gift from God like everything else is, so one day we will go home and meet God face to face.

I feel in my heart God and I are basically the same like two sides of a coin.

Forget the past or you will never have a future. Do not look back. You have to develop your own meditative mind.

God gave us the power to desire; but whatever you desire you should be able to control it.

Always give yourself a chance. Count your dimension and always direct your energy in God's way. You will find peace, happiness, prosperity and joy,

To understand your existence, Know you are honest, to speak the truth because we were born with the truth.

When you sit in a room with other people and you talk about God, love and elevation, that is when you manifest God.

We can all do wrong. But we can try and do it right. In my heart I don't believe we should kill or punish a person; find wrong and make it right. This is called the flow of life.

I pray one day we will all be awakened to a higher consciousness.

Always know you are the Will of God. I am God.

Getting up in the morning is a selfish act, but it is a personal strength for sharpness and discipline.

You always heard life is a play, but your mission in life, to understand that whatever you do to keep guiding all coming generations.

Trust in God As you dwell in God.

Self-discipline is not a project. You must have discipline or you may grow up the wrong way.

Love yourself so you will have freedom, liberation, and ecstasy. Accept your life is very sacred. Prayer is power and so is love.

We are all part of the universe and the magnetic field. The way we feel is our choice that matters and God's plan.

Religion is a family of God; religion is a state of consciousness.

If this religion does the job, How can you be depressed all together?

Forgiveness is the highest performance and the direct approach to life.

If something is wrong don't let it remain wrong.

To achieve a desire you have to have commitment and the will to do it.

May God guide you, protect you, that you grow in grace. May you shine like the sun and know all.

When you are spiritual do not react or be afraid.

Remember you are what you relate to, don't limit yourself or you will be limited.

Universal, Obey, serve and love. Religions will change; prophets will come and go, merge in God and obey this law.

Pray for peace strength and grace.

Leave your problems, serve Uplift others.

If you are positive you have the power to think who you really are and what you can be.

When that special moment comes listen and know and be the truth.

Everyone has been blessed in body, mind, and soul. This is the highest. This is the highest your body, mind can serve the soul.

Everyone has a bright beautiful soul. All you have to do is get in touch with it.

Sometimes we are tested in life to let your standards be tested.

See God in all; and serve God in all.

Life is a gift that lives on.

Any challenge in life has to be met. It is a test of the human dignity.

This life is not about you. It is about your spirit.

If you have fear or are afraid, say "no." God will take care of you. Trust God.

Wisdom becomes knowledge, just know it.

Things may change in your life whatever it may be. What you wear, eating habits, social behavior and your destiny.

In the Age of Aquarius everyone will be the leader of his or her own spirit. You will be in control of your own life.

I pray every day that God will raise us up higher and higher, to give us the strength and courage to be humble to serve and reach out to all.

There is good and bad in the world but choose the right way with a smile and grace, that people know they can trust you.

Just as marriage is an exalted state to be in where two people become One Divine Being.

When you take time to meditate you can empty yourself and let the Universe come to you.

To serve mankind we should use our present hospitality and service to serve all mankind with grace and love.

When you think with your head, think with your heart. When you think with your heart, think with your head.

I pray to God to bless us and rise above everything that we can, serve, be truthful, humble, strong and smile to make this a better world.

Did you ever ask yourself who you are? You are a human being. "HU" means spirit, the light and "Man" means mental. You are the spirit of your mind, the bright light of yourself. But it seems I am a mortal being. You are a mortal being if you know you are God, you are free.

Two ways to live in this world, worry or relax. If you worry you have to concentrate it is physical, use your mind to the Universal Mind things will come to you. "This is true."

Whenever you receive a gift, thank God it becomes of fate. If you do not give thanks it becomes a curse.

Note that we all were born with "X" amount of breath. But if you breathe faster, you will lose your life earlier.

If you see someone falling apart try to keep them together. Just don't let him fall, and that way you can keep yourself from falling.

Always try to meditate on God to transform himself from "I" to "We" in the life here, and the where after.

You can lose weight by working on your metabolism and your glandular system, get started with a guru or yoga teacher.

You should have self-knowledge like lighting a candle. Once you light it all darkness goes away. Just love yourself, and then you can love everyone.

God is within you. Our God will not abandon you even if He wants to.

When we are still and silent you can receive all knowledge.

To have knowledge is to develop faith in yourself.

You should have enough grace in your heart to fill this entire Universe. Like the smell of a rose it is so powerful, but your grace should be so powerful that people want to feel it.

Jesus Christ said you should have enough faith as a mustard seed. Be firm in your faith. Do everything with love.

When two people are in a relationship there should not be any agony. You should honor your word. Don't exploit each other. Be kind and gentle. You took a vow to respect it.

Hugging is so good for the soul. If you cannot hug yourself, you cannot hug another.

CHAPTER 8

"My Experiences"

Only read books that people have had experience with.

My first experience was at seven years old when I made my first communion. I did not believe in confession.

When I was nine years old my grandma was cleaning her dresser drawer, as I was sitting on the bed watching her I saw a rosary and a prayer book. I said, "Grandma when you die, will you send me three roses so I know you are in heaven?" Thirteen years later my husband and I went to breakfast over to my parents. I rang the bell and my mom came to the door with the Sunday paper. My mom said, "Look at this. A man got up in the morning and when he was coming down his living room steps, he saw three roses on his living room floor, but did not know how they got there." But through this man the media my mom I knew my grandma was in heaven. It took three people to get in touch with me through the spirit world.

I woke up in the middle of the night and I was cold so I said I wish I had a blanket. All of a sudden I felt this energy go over me and I fell asleep.

A friend of mine of over thirty years was eighty-two and still working. She asked me to make two keys for her and bring them over on Monday because her children were coming from out of town and she was going to the hospital on Tuesday. I told my mom if something good doesn't happen. She will commit suicide.

On Monday I tried to get the key made three times but something always came up. I did get the keys made and went over about 3:00 p.m. We had dinner together and I said I'd see you in the hospital.

She said to wait. I got a social security card in the mail with her name but her husband's number on it. If you are losing it why would you get a social security card at eighty-two years old? I called social security and the man told me it was a mystery.

I took the card and put it on the table and all of a sudden I got all this energy and I said, "Your husband is with us right here to my right side. I feel his presence." I had so much energy I could have taken her house right off the foundation. I kept saying, "Do you feel his presence?"

But I think she must have thought I'd lost it. I took her hand, she was levitating. She stood in front of me and I looked t her face and her white hair was brown and like a pageboy cut.

I took my hand away and she sat down and said why did he wait so long and pills were not a way out. That night in bed I was just filled with a lot of energy and fell asleep,

One summer we were at my parent's house. We had a cookout and when everyone left, it was evening already. I took a bath. When I got out of the tub to dry myself off I felt hands on my shoulder. But I was alone in the bathroom. I just had a towel around me, and the hands on my shoulders moved me out of the bathroom, down the hallway into the bedroom and put me right in front of the dresser where I had my jewelry box and my wedding rings were missing.

I started to cry and went into this living room where both my parents were sitting and I said someone took my wedding rings.

I called my friend and she did a reading for me—the drawing was a house with a lot of steps, and the rings would be in a vase on top of a refrigerator. I had my dad take me to this person's house and he tried to get her out of the kitchen but it did not work out. But months later a friend of mine told me this person had wedding rings for sale.

My friend said another teacher is coming through in tulip time. Good things will come to you. And I will always be on the inside looking out.

Some friends moved away, and it was only a half-year later and I felt her husband needed prayers. So every morning when I had breakfast and prayed for the world, I would pray for him. Two weeks later I got a letter. Her husband needed surgery, and took a test first. I knew it was your prayers.

About two and a half years after I was married I was lying in bed alone. My son of two months was in the crib and my German Shepard dog was next to the crib. I looked over to my right side and I saw a dark form of a person standing next to me. The whole room was a dead still. At first, I thought it was my father-in-law because we lived in the back house. It just stood there and left. Six months later I got a divorce.

One year later I saw it again, but it kept coming to me but it was always there for me when something was going on in my life.

Later on I married an older man and told him about it but he could never see it—this person was there before I had surgery a few times.

I always heard a dark person is on the negative side so I went to a preacher and he said Satan takes this form of a person. He was coming more and more. After six years I willed it away. But no harm ever came to me. I'm sure that when the time comes I will find out who this person was.

One evening I was taking a bath and I was in a twilight sleep and sliding under the water. All of a sudden I felt someone take my arm and pulled me up real quick before I went under and I thanked them.

I volunteered at this one hospital twenty—five years. One night while I was in the gift shoppe, a lady came in and she was crying. I asked if I cold help her. She said her dad was in the hospital, but it was her husband. She said he was from another country and their son was in college and was very hard on him. I said if your husband does not change his ways, your son will commit suicide,

The one group home where I worked and you could hear children running around and some aides would see a woman in a gown walking the halls at night. A Lot of strange things happened.

But it used to be an old farmhouse and a barn outside next to a park.

After my sister passed away her daughter had a little girl years later. She was now two years old. We all were at an outing. Everyone went into the house and I was with her daughter. She was in a walker. All of a sudden she looked at me, started to come toward me and her hands and arms were moving so fast I got scared. I could not believe she was doing like she was telling me I was your sister. But the whole family feels the same way and even her daughter. She was moving all different ways that she wanted my attention. With her arms waving all over she got my attention.

I started to be different age seven when I had my first Holy Communion and confession. I did not believe in confession.

At age nine my grandma was cleaning the dresser drawer out and she put a prayer book and rosary on the bed. Out of the blue, I said, "Grandma when you die, send me three roses so I know you are in heaven."

It was on a Sunday, my husband and I went to my parents for breakfast My mom came to the door with the Sunday paper and told mother a man was going down his stairs to his living room when he found three roses on the floor. He did not know how they got there. I told my grandma, this man and through now you I know grandma is in heaven. It took thirteen years for grandma to let me know and it went through three other people.

A friend of mine was having a barbeque built to get this one man he is really good. After a few hours on the job he asked my friend for $500,00 more for material he needed. He took the money and left. My friend called the police, but everyone was looking for him, even the State Patrol. I started to pray every morning. God never made a dishonest or greedy man and my friend could not be a victim of anyone's dishonest or greed. That divine love met and always will meet any human need. I prayed for a little over a year, and one week I went out to his house. It was on a Thursday and I said, "You are getting the money back this weekend." He just looked at me. It was on a Saturday night at 6:30 p.m., a knock at the door. A police officer handed him an envelope with $500.00. He had turned himself in.

We are all connected in some way. Like two friends of mine moved away, it was about one and a half years later, one morning while having my breakfast I pray for the world and all concerned. I knew a friend needed prayers. I prayed for one week. Two weeks later I got a letter from his wife. I knew it was your prayers. Her husband had to have tests before he surgery and they said he didn't need surgery now. And I knew it was your prayers. She once told me she did not believe in God. Her mother went for help to the church but she was turned down and committed suicide. But after the time I was with her she started believing again.

At the group home I took my friend's dog to visit the people once in awhile and the dog would go b everyone but when I went by this one little lady who was over eighty years old the stood like a statute and would not move. I knew this woman had some psychic ability. When I started to leave and say good-bye. Here she was standing by the door. I was shocked to see her standing there. Al of a sudden I looked into her face and I heard a woman's voice saying, "Get me out of here" and kept repeating it. Her hair was brown and cut like a pageboy. I said God what can I do. She's in this home. I kept hearing "Get me out of here." Now this woman was over eighty years old with white short hair.

She never talked and you had to help her walk to the chair or table. This happened again and I asked God, what can I do for her and the other people? This woman who owned the group home was starving the people and much more, so I reported her. She was closed down and this lady was moved out to a better place, plus the other residents were moved elsewhere.

My friend Aggie opened a bakery in an old building on the south side of Milwaukee. A family, husband, wife, son and daughter went up north. On the way home he was going to beat the train but the train beat him and the whole family died. Now when we are there as I help her out at times we have seen the little girl and present the presence of a large man in back of me in he basement. One of the girls came in at five a.m. to start work. She heard some noise and the little girl Lory and a dress and said to her "Am I Dead?" She didn't know what to say. I told her next time you see her tell her, "Yes, go home." The other help see her too. She is about 8 or 9 years old. Then again a large person put their hands on my shoulder.

I went to the club where I go and this couple were dancing. When they came off he floor, I told my mom that man is going to die soon. Two weeks later I heard he was in his garden, went inside to rest and died. It was just two weeks.

One time we were at a festival and these children were playing this golf game, a hole in one. No one was getting the ball in. A half an hour went by and this young girl came to try. I told myself she will do it and she did.

When my mom broke her hip, she had to go to a nursing home for awhile for rehab. The second night there she was having dinner and said she needed her sweater. I told her I would get it on the way back. This lady who was taking care of another woman asked my why my mom was there. I said while we were at a theater she went to the bathroom and felt she was going to fall. But when she came out, the thought of her falling left. When she got to the row we were sitting in, she fell, and I felt really bad. So this lady said, "What to you see in me and no one ever said that to me.: She said it again and I did not answer the third time. She stood right in front of me and demanded I tell her this never happened to me before. All of a sudden, I saw an aura behind her. I started to tell her many things that were not good. She said she was kicking her boyfriend out, etc. But I heard later she went back to her old ways.

My friend who adopted me in her heart brought me up with Edgar Cayce. It made my life much better and different ways of thinking and for the healing I got from her and those in the spirit world and from Edgar Cayce.

My friend said she is coming back to me through a trumpet.

She also said everyone will be a golden tan in the future.

I was told to take my money out of he bank. In the future it won't be any good.

I was cleaning the oven and I picked up the burner and it was still hot. All I cold think of was my friend. She said think of my brother. He was killed in a fire. Call me back in fifteen minutes. When I called her back she said an Indian was standing at her side from the spirit world. I looked at my hand. The burn was gone and no more pain in my hand. My friend was Indian and French.

ESP Extra sensory perception, awareness of or response to our external or influence not apprehended by sensory means.

A Telepathy, Thought, Transference.
B Clairvoyance; The power of discerning.
C Precognition; Seeing the future.
D Post recognition; seeing into the past.
E Psychogeneses; The effect of he mind on an object.

This is how my friend told me about ESP.

My friend gave me this prayer to say. This is a beautiful Sioux Indian prayer. Oh Great Spirit whose voice I hear in the winds, and whose breath gives life to the entire world, hear me. I come before you one of your many children. I am small and weak. I need your strength and wisdom. Let me walk in beauty and make my eyes ever behold the red purple sunset. Make my hands respect the things you have taught my people. The lessons you have hidden in every leaf and rock. I seek strength not to be superior to my people, but to be able to fight my greatest enemy, myself. Make me ever ready to come to you with clean hands and straight eyes, so when life fades as a fading sunset, my spirit may come to you without shame. Amen.

It was springtime around 9:30 p.m. I was in bed. I turned over and I saw this dark form of a person standing next to the bed and I thought someone was playing a joke on me. I was very calm and the whole room was like a dead still. I knew it was someone from the sprit world. It stayed for about ten minutes. A year later, I went through a divorce. All went well, then this black form of a person came to me again and I would see it in the hallway. When I went through surgery, I saw this person all the time. I remarried and I would ask my husband there is that person, can you see it? This went on for about five years. One day I felt it was with me every time I went through different things in my life and I knew it would not harm me. But this church next door where we lived, I thought I would talk to the preacher. He said it was "Satan" so my thoughts changed and I willed it away. But to me that was a big mistake I made. I tried to will this person back but this person never came back to guide me again.

A friend of mine invited me to his home but said to come on Friday and leave Saturday. I said, "No, I want to come on Thursday and leave Friday." I finally agreed to come on Friday and leave Saturday. I had a dream three days before I was going to his house. I was going under a bridge, my car got out of control, spun around a few times and went under the bridge and scraped the whole front end. I got out of the car. I saw the car was white and I was not hurt.

I went to my friend's house on Friday and left Saturday. On the expressway the dream came true. The car got out of control. I must have hit some black ice on the expressway. My car spun, hit the side of the bridge, and scraped the whole front end. I got out. I was ok; saw it was a white car I just bought new three days ago. But I could not figure out this busy highway was like a dead still around me. For about twelve to fifteen minutes there were no cars on the highway, as if God had stopped all the traffic.

CHAPTER 9

Yoga

Yoga is the oldest science to man. Yoga is for women, men, children for any age. When you define Yoga, it is unity or joining together.

Using age as an excuse is only a state of mind.

Yoga is derived from the Sanskrit root meaning bind yoke-it is a union of our will and the will of God, yoking all the powers of the body, mind and soul to God. It mans disciplining of he intellect. It means a poise of the soul which enables one to look at life in all its aspects evenly.

It is not a religion in itself. It is a way of life so you can attain a deeper, fuller understanding of your own religious beliefs.

Yoga brings health and well being to each individual. Yoga tones the body and will give you more energy, vitality and an overall improvement in good health looks. Yoga is the understanding the human form and how to preserve the health and youthfulness of one's self.

Its through yoga that you will gain the knowledge to create the happy, healthy body and mind.

Meditation is a powerful tool for quieting the mind and effortlessly turns back towards itself.

Edgar Cayce, who was a great prophet and psychic, called it the "Magic-silence) potent silence. Twenty minutes in the morning and twenty minutes in the evening.

Breathing: breath unlocks the power of energy when the body opens the channels to replenish the flow of external energy to learn to breath is to learn to live.

Breath gets rid of tension and many other problems. There are over 100 ways to breath. Breath cures all.

Through yoga many things happen when you have spiritual powers. You shine like the sun and know all, but you must use these powers in the right way.

Everything is a state of mind. This world is only an illusion, only a dream.

When your mind is truthful all your actions will bear positive fruit immediately.

When a man lives and entertains the truth alone, he becomes a source of enlightenment to all others.

Everything we experience is the self. Tell yourself you are aware of the self and who you are.

Yoga can bring internal harmony and control over the nervous system and conservation of energy. It will develop poise, balance, flexibility and ability to relax. It will give you a better outlook ion life, better health. Your attitude has everything to do with your life, so when a negative thought comes into your mind, right away change it to a positive one or the problem will just get bigger.

Just as bitterness and anger stop the flow of energy and destroy the cells. Anxiety stress is based on belief of limitations.

We do yoga, that is a storehouse of impressions, can be burnt up. As we need grace from a great being. We all need the grace of God.

We all need self-discipline, meditating ego and renunciation.

By purifying the mind one starts to know the nature of God.

Go on beyond your fears, conflicts and desires so you can experience the Self within.

Yoga strengthens the body and mind. And your body has a pattern of its own and established ageing process. Yoga makes people live longer. Yoga stimulates abdominal muscles, spine, lungs, pelvic area, refreshes the glands and nerve centers with pranic energy from the disciplined breathing. Yoga therapy automatically brings into being a state of mind perfectly attend his own psychoanalyst. Yoga is a union of body and mind.

When the breath is irregular the mind is unsteady. When you breath is still so is the mind. Still yoga obtains the power of stillness.

The (asonas postures) will refine your inner and outer spaces, as well as harmonize life giving systems of he body. When you think you can't do any more with the body, you can still get breath benefits in just a few postures. This (asonas postures) is to restore energy.

As you sow, so shall you reap.

Every thing that we do is the fruit of our experiences.

Become liberated while living. Perform your duty. Don't worry about the future.

When you practice yoga, every move takes you through a limitation to a new sense of freedom. The practice of yoga is to merge this illusionary self, the ego or self. That is why man is subject to eternal "births and deaths." Because man's idea is to attempt to satisfy and fulfill itself. The meaning of yoga is to go merge the illusionary self with the ocean of universal mind. So cause and effect cease to be a reality and true peace is experienced. To achieve this liberation we engage in the practices of both physical and mental.

There is no such thing as failure in yoga, just degrees of success. This success depends on time and effort you devote to your practice. The more you practice the greater will be your advancement. Yoga and meditation you are making a very wise decision. Many things can happen through yoga.

The left force in you when in the company of certain people, those who do not have their own organisms, draw on the vitality of those around them. Be with people who have much more life force than yourself. Idle chatter is a way to use up your life force. We talk a lot but say very little. Some people depend on the TV, or radio to keep their senses occupied. Don't worry what other people think of you. Just pay attention to your own emotional body. Too much TV, movies, computers, newspapers, magazines, murder sin, etc. The entertainment makes you restless, tense and emotionally strained and drained. So many things in life today take your energy. You should try to avoid it whenever possible.

Yoga philosophy and Meditation

Yoga is man's oldest known method of scientifically dealing with the self. You waste your life force by nervous habits, being with negative people, idle talk, misuse of your senses, smoking, pacing, chewing gum and many other useless actions, expression of fear, anger, anxiety and other unhealthy mental emotional conditions.

You have to learn to relax with your activities. Haven't you always heard, make every move count? Take lessons from the cat, his moves, stretches, relaxes, and naps. The cat does not waste energy. But you can learn from him about conservation.

Everyone wants to be happy and get the most out of life. We want contentment and peace of mind and soul. But unhappiness and discontentment are all around us. Money and fame do not bring us closer to the peace within us that we seek.

Sometimes we go through life in what seems to promise relief. But sooner or later none of these things can help us with the ultimate peace that we seek all these things and are substitutes. It attempts to treat the symptoms, not the real cause. If we have peace of mind, body and spirit we could pierce through the heart of the matter.

Though yoga we learn different levels of consciousness and sub consciousness.

Yoga explains there is also a higher or super consciousness that we refer to as universal mind. All problems, confusion, suffering in life stem from the fact that we do not understand the nature of our ordinary mind, that we possess the power of the Universal Mind. Ordinary mind has taken over our lives. It is our higher consciousness that we find ourselves in the most perplexing circumstances beset by problems which seem to be no solution.

Some of us are not aware of the existence of the Universal Mind and do not know how to use it.

Use your mind to lead you down the path of faith, peace and fulfillment. Don't chase after empty promises. Keep hoping for success. If you have not fulfilled yourself it can lead you to blame any and every conceivable outside circumstances. Then you say its bad luck. You fail because it is misunderstood working of our ordinary mind.

Everyone is looking for that pot of gold at the end of he rainbow. What we see is part of a circle. In yoga we use the symbol of a wheel that we call he wheel of life. Each of us has to pass through all of the possible conditions of the human existence, night and day and drink the waters that truly satisfy thirst.

ALL TRUTH AND WISDOM ARE UNIVERSAL MIND

Some people don't think that the ordinary mind creates our problems and then in its own good time, solves them on the outside. So is a game that will continue to prey long as you allow it to do so. With meditation you will come to understand that your are not your ordinary mind and that it has not nearly the importance which we attach to it.

Knowing how to concentrate will open up new facilities of the mind; give you insight on how to accomplish what you must with a minimum effort.

When you have extra hours don't clutter your mind with idle daydreams, wishful thinking or the past or the future. It is an illusionary flash way to see the world and ourselves in relation to it. It takes a lot of life force to think the mind is like a record that plays over and over again. Meditate during your daily activities; try to withdraw yourself from this world of activity for a period of time each day.

You have to become the master of your mind and not the slave. It has to take orders, not give them. You have to understand yourself, to find peace of mind and spirit to lead to a richer life.

We have to catch the body from being tense, unnecessarily strained as it is drawing our vital energies. We have to learn that the ordinary mind is needlessly sapping our life force by allowing it to run wild without control. Observe your mind. Notice if it has been concentrated on what you're doing.

Yoga has changed people's lives from the ancient science, which restores health, vigor and youth. Yoga is a physical and spiritual experience. Yoga can build and restore vitality, body harmony and keeping you young. Yoga is a branch of the Hindu philosophy. I am glad one of my teachers was the first who brought yoga to the states. India is the land of its origin.

Many men and women in movies of the Western world stood on their heads and did yoga. If you are a Jew, Christian or whatever, yoga does not have an affect on one's own faith. Just as holding the breath you can recharge he body. Just by holding the breath and you feel a little lightheaded, this can open your psychic development. Yogis become clairvoyant through concentrating on recharging the body.

Meditating on the true self and dreams many things come true through my dreams. Using the word Om, supreme word of God, signifying all of nature as the universe—a sacred word which you can meditate on.

"Just as a man must raise himself by is own efforts, be his own friend, or he alone is his worst enemy."

Many of the exercises combined with the breathing build up resistance and relieve certain psychosomatic symptoms.

Past lives for some misfortunes or evil, the better ones left, the higher the development next time around.

Watch your thoughts. It is not far away. But be careful what you wish for, even your parents. Some people do not believe after death we return again. I believe my sister who passed on came back and her daughter now is her mother.

Healing people from miles away just by meditating and prayer can heal them. Some friends of mine moved miles away and it was little over a year and one morning while having breakfast I felt he needed prayers. I prayed every morning for a week. Two weeks later I got a letter in the mail from his wife saying the morning he was to have surgery. They took a test and he did not need the surgery. I knew it was your prayers. Prayer is powerful.

We should think more of the beauty around us and in every form, nature and of people and their problems.

We should think more of the universe around its wonders—the animals, flowers, and trees and us have their place in the natural rhythm of life.

Always stay in tune with the universe and God. The effort you make to find yourself with your own faith will be its own reward.

Yoga can do a lot for you. You will be less critical, have more compassion, be more understanding, smile and be more open to others.

Reincarnation—People know that life does not begin at birth or end at death. It is the acts we have previous existences.

Meditating on God, I know all things are possible for God, and then possible for me to finish this life before the new kingdom comes in 20112.

Man was and is a mysterious marvel, between time and space. We have to awake and get out of the slumber, the power limitlessness of the SELF.

Everyone struggles for health to conquer the body and soul. It is like a flower unfolding. Then letting the sunshine come in. Some people keep blinders on of all material things. Then those who are more spiritual for a more beautiful and higher life. They say the greatest mind on earth is man.

Man has tried to solve that mystery and the greatest secret there is; but the self.

Just as Hatha Yoga "Ha Sun" "the Moon" "Joining" "Yoke" it is the perfect knowledge of the two energies, positive sun and the negative moon energies joining in perfect harmony

Hatha Yoga helps us to utilize and store the free flow of the life force to the maximum extent. Since man is spirit clothed in flesh and within himself he reflects the laws of spirit and body.

Positive energy is life giving. Heavy eating and drinking, the physical side causes of obesity and mental obtuseness that upset the individual's equilibrium.

Some people do not believe a higher self that opens the way for the eternal source of strength that dwells within their soul. Some people lack self-confidence, and then he becomes powerless and helpless.

You will succeed if you believe in what you are doing and have enough self-confidence to master all difficulties.

The greatest teacher in the world is Jesus Christ. Remember what he said, who came out of the east. "Take no thought for your life, that what ye shall eat or what ye shall drink; nor yet for your body, what ye shall put on. Is not the life more than meat, and body more than raiment? Behold the fowls of the air; for they sow not, neither do they reap, nor gather into bins; yet your heavenly Father feedeth them. Are ye not much better than they?"

I saw Jesus Christ in a dream. Beautiful.

Our minds collect data from reincarnations. But we are here now to better ourselves, our personality and higher self.

Hatha Yoga shows us how to keep order from the forces that animate the body, that we have sinned against our health. Through yoga, you can start a better healthy you. Open yourself to a higher awareness psychic enfoldment to control your life and your world as never before. Get rid of fear, sins and mental blocks. Free yourself now.

A Yoga pose MATSYDSANA Matsya means fish. Matsya the fish incarnation of Visnu, the source and maintainer of the universe and of all things. It is related that once upon a time the whole earth had become corrupt and was about to be overwhelmed by a universal flood. Visnu took the form of a fish and warned Manu the Hindu Adam of the impending disaster. The fish carried Manu, his family and the seven great sages in a ship, fastened to a horn on his head. It also saved the Veda from the flood.

We are all connected in some way.

Meditation releases you of all tension, distress—take deep breathe through the nose, take a deep breath expanding your consciousness. Close your eyes in concentration, relax the mind. Open your heart to Christ's presence and his angels of light.

Relax. Let go. Now rest in god's love and peace nourishing the spirit within this blessing and rest cleanses and steadies the mind uplifting and healing your spirit within.

"Now you are everywhere, everything."

You should get a good Guru or teacher to help you with yoga and breathing.

One who practices kundalini yoga, 108 elements in the universe including a conscious creation of the Creator.

Kundalini Yoga is not a religion; religions came out of it. Kundalini Yoga is not a fad, not a cult. It is a practice of experience of a person's own dormant excellence that is awakened.

We are now entering the Age of Aquarius. It will be a new time. The entire psyche is changing. You must purify your mind, body and soul to be real. You have to elevate yourself to be angelic. This age will serve us in an age of awareness and experience.

Humming the word OM you will experience a different sound and vibrations and begin to say it faster and faster. Just the word OM with humming sound calms the mind, opens the brain waves to reach out into the universe, everything comes from the word OM, or springs from the word OM.

Healing the wounds of love, love is life; it brings us to life, gives us courage to live our life. It inspires us to sacrifice our life for others. As natural as love is so are the wounds of live. Live carefully. You need to learn how to heal the wounds of love. You have to heal old wounds which were broken.

You start your morning with a cup of joy. Tell yourself I'm Happy. I'm Healthy. I'm Holy. Start seeing good in yourself and the universe.

Unfold peace and harmony. Be careful who your friends are. They reflect you and you reflect them.

Bow to yourself and thank yourself.

Keep your mind under control at all times, no matter how things go. You must remain calm, quiet and peaceful. That peace is the source of prosperity. It is the highest spiritual strength. There is nothing to match it. Don't run away from your problems. Face it. Say this is my fear. I am afraid of this fear. It will melt away into nothingness.

The past is dead this is the present and the future will take care of itself.

Keep your mind under control. By letting go it all gets done. This world was won by those who let go. But when you try and try, it is even be on the winning.

Some people have a chip on their shoulder. People should behave rightly toward the rest of the world.

Fill your cup. Yesterday that seemed not important exist not. You should fill your cup with love of life and success. Forget the failures and trials that were burned yesterday. The future will take care of itself.

My sister gave me a cup of soup and I returned the cup empty. So she called me and said you did not fill the cup. I said God can fill it with al lot more than I can. Three hours later she called me and said we just sold our house. I said, "See. I told you God can fill it more than I can.

Just be relaxed and free and God will work wonders for thee.

2012
The end of a new beginning.
We have to get back to God.
The only miracle is unity!

CHAPTER 10

Dreams

Almost all of my dreams are in color. Edgar Cayce came to me many times. One time he told me to pray for this country. In another dream he came back and told me to pray for the tribes. When people come to you from the spirit world they tell you different ways how they cam across. Like my friend, she would do drawings and hearts or circles, would be the months. The readings were very beautiful drawings that she did. As for myself when I see people I just tell them whoever is coming through me from the spirit world.

I had this dream that lasted three nights of the same two men in that dream.

I saw Jesus Christ in a dream. He is very beautiful and he came closer and closer to me.

A Guru in my dream carried me over a stream to his room and said it is small because were are only here for a short time. He took me back to the stream and on my right side, I saw these people with white clothes on and it was very peaceful and beautiful.

I hope this is going to be like 2012.

In the dream there were three Indians. Two were on horseback with their beautiful headdresses and the clothes they had on were riding off. They turned around and kept going but the third Indian was sitting on the ground. He was an old chief with a beautiful headdress on. He said he was tired so I sat with him.

My sister called me and told me my friend Beaver died. He killed himself. A few weeks later he came to me in a dream and said someone had a gun to his head (a figure of speech). He was so pure and alight around him. But three months later he came back to me and said everything is ok.

Months after my husband died he came to me in a dream. We were in a car by a bridge and we got out and see him hanging over the bridge with just his hands holding on. I just stood awhile and at first I did not want to do it. But I took his fingers off the bridge so he could not hold on any more, to let go. And that was the end of the dream. But for the last ten years he was attached to the earth planet.

One dream I saw a girl, very beautiful with blonde hair. I asked her name because my friend said my angel would be a girl. She said her name was Alison.

In one dream a voice told me theosone for epilepsy. TheoO means "God." "Shane means "natural," a friend of mine who brought yoga to the states told me.

One dream was in a swimming pool. I was holding this young boy about eight years old. Front of his body was in my arms. Just then the phone rang and I said, "Hello, Hello." There was a lot of static on the phone and loud. I kept saying "hello." Then a man's voice said it was in the lining. He said Good Night. I never have heard a voice that different and pure. I called the ARE Clinic and talked to a few different people and one man said we were always wondering what Edgar Cayce meant by talking to people in the spirit world. I'll never forget that voice. As my friend said, we would talk to our loved ones through a phone.

In this one dream I was in a hallway with other people and there was a fire with a lot of flame. Everyone was trying to get out. I was the last one. When I was going through the fire, it wasn't a fire at all. It was my thoughts only saw silver or aluminum foil.

One dream IO was swimming in a pool. When I got to the end of the pool, my whole body went up in the air about six feet, halfway across the pool and back into the water.

I fly a lot in my dreams, even if it is from one block to the next.

If you want to contact someone in the spirit world, hold both thumbs.

IO dreamt of Michel Landon from Little House on the Prairie. He was sitting by a window just looking out. He looked at peace

I dreamt of Elvis Presley a few months after he died. He was walking on a beach.

In November of 1987 I dreamt of peace in the world.

Gail Cayce and her dad came to my home where I used to live when I was 17.

1-7-81 I was at a birthday and my grandma was with us, but already was gone.

2-26-81 The dream was the Atlanta, Georgia killings and I saw the person who did it.

2-27-81 Bob Hope was in a dream a few times. James Cagney was in a dream.

7-15-81 I found a silver cross with a Madonna on it.

9-30-81 Sylvester Stallone we were very happy and he was very nice to me.

When I went to pay my food bill, I saw a picture of Linda Evans, a girl who married the entertainer and I knew they would break up two weeks later. They did.

JR from Dallas was losing everything. Pam was in the dream.

1-12-81 Natalie Wood. I saw just her head lying there.

1-14-82 Paul Lynn was sitting with me when I was at the Performing Arts Center.

1-27-82 Frank from Hill Street Blues

10-5-82 Bing Crosby

1-10-83 Shirley on TV from Laverne and Shirley

3-27-83 Phil Donahue show

4-5-83 An angel of mercy came to me three times.

4-8-83 Prince Charles' Diane was pregnant. It was a false pregnancy.

5-22-83 I saw two books by July 6. Gold old fashioned cover three inches high and an old fashioned lady on the cover. They were books for the future to communicate with the spirit world, for telephones for the spirit world.

2-10-82 I saw a lot of war equipment. Reds?

2-28-82 A basketball team was going on strike.

3-11-82 I was in an old house from 1800 to 1900. One room is where a man died.

4-23-82 I saw the girl on the Charmin tissue. I saw her parents.

6-2-82 I was in the service. I told my Sgt about a nuclear war.

7-2-82 I was in a church with a microchip. Some men were after me for it. It could blow up the world. I handed it to the priest. It was silver with dots or holes 2X2 wrapped around it.

8-8-83 I dreamt of my dad. He had a green shirt on and kissed me. Then he passed out all these gifts at Xmas.

2-15-84 I saw three flying saucers all around the sky and one split into two. One a bright light and round on more with a light went under water and the water got real high. My friend told me I would see three flying saucers. That was in 1963.

3-2-86 I had two pots of chili on the stove. They floated to the ground.

8-5-86 The Bermuda triangle is a dangerous place. A turtle told me this turtle was in my dream. I kept him warm and fed him.

4-29-89 I was flying all around in my dream.

10-31-94 Edgar Cayce came to me and again told me to bless this country. I woke up at 6:30 a.m. right after he told me this. I felt his presence on my left side.

7-20-97 My sister-in-law was in a nursing home. I went to visit her. She was in a wheelchair. Two days later I dreamt of her in a dream in the wheelchair. She stood up and floated away. I called my friend who ran the home. I said did my sister-in-law pass away at 1 a.m. in the morning. She said yes. It was beautiful and spiritual.

5-20-84 I dreamt I left but came back to earth to live with peace and love, and harmonize and beautify fields with others.

In a dream I was to leave this earth planet but I said "no" not yet.

I dreamt three days before my friend wanted me to come over on Friday and leave Saturday. He said come Thursday and leave Friday. In my dream I was in a white car, went under a bridge. It spun around, went under the bridge and the front of the car hit the inside of the bridge. I got out and was not hurt but looked at the car. It was white. I went to his house on Friday, left Saturday. The whole dream came true just what I saw in the dream. But I was on the expressway all the time it happened. Until I got help no others came by.

4-8-97 Abraham Lincoln looked like he was 5' 3" and thin. I touched his feet and he was funny.

8-31-92 I saw Cleopatra in Rome. There was a little boy in bed and he said he was sick and dying. He had another brother. He was the better one. I saw pink ashes and I touched them.

9-26-79 I saw a WFO in the sky with beautiful lights and stars and water.

8-20-89 I was in another country. This lady told me she was leaving this earth planet in six hours and I was to wear a white blouse.

1-4-90 Chippewa Falls. I saw part of a plane that fell to the ground and hit a silo in a field. No one was hurt.

2-6-90 I was in a church. This priest gave me five dollars to light five candles. Then a group of us turned around and sang Silent Night. One lady had a beautiful voice.

5-25-90 I dreamt of a man doing Kratel and knogfer. All he said was two words—Tie Lee.

6-3-88 I could will animals and when I told someone else to look at them they would disappear, a lion or tiger.

8-10-88 I was looking at a lady who passed away, lying in a coffin. She got up and walked away with her husband.

I dreamt of my husband and his family smiling, but the next day his son died.

11-11-88 I dreamt of my friend's sister who wanted me to come over to the spirit world. I told her "no" not yet.

11-15-88 Elvis, I was with Elvis Presley when we were standing and talking. He was at peace. He had something in his hand and gave it away.

9-16-87 I was sitting by a swimming pool in a chair. All of a sudden I started floating across the swimming pool. I did it two times. This one woman said it was impossible.

11-13-87 Peace. I was playing a song on the tape recorder. I saw the sun and clouds went over me. Then I saw the sky light up. The water became very high. It had to be in the East.

3-6-87 I dreamt I was in a car accident and saw people from another planet. Then I met this woman who was from another planet but spoke another language. But I could understand her. It was an easy language and very beautiful surroundings.

3-18-87 My friend pushed me away until I told her what happened about her husband. But I cannot remember anything. She was standing by the window.

4-25-87 I was to meditate on prosperity. Then I was told every thousand years, this was the day to ask for anything.

1-9-87 This man was doing surgery on this other man. His eyes were large and green, hypnotizing him. There was a lot of blood and when it was over, the blood stopped and was gone. He said everything was ok.

9-14-86 I dreamt of Hitler and his wife.

4-24-86 Healing, meditating on the color red and getting rid of a gland, etc., then change it to blue.

4-7-86 My death. I could not get a full breath. It took a long time and it was very short. That was the end of that life. I was not afraid. I felt peace within me. No fear.

2-7-86 An astrologer woman was in my dream and said don't cry. Read the stars and I would be changing planes or trains.

1-10-85 There was a man named "Ramatha" who foretold the future. I was in France. This woman told me to take a deep breath. I said I want to see "Ramtha". All of a sudden he appeared with a gold and black crown.

1-10-85 I needed more proof with a gust of wind I almost fell over. I knew it was Ramtha. I looked out to the window and saw trucks and trains falling over but I knew no one was hurt. Then the train came through the side of the house but no one was hurt. I guess he was trying to prove to me who he was. I made the sign of the cross. First I touched my tongue. Before Ramtha was just a form of a person.

5-22-86 I saw Gandhi in my dream.

1-31-85 My dad's sister came to me, touched my hand and said good things will come to me.

2-10-2002 My friend's husband was in a dream. He re-enacted my daughter's death.

4-4-03 My mom was in a nursing home and my sister, who passed away, said the lady running the home was at fault. My mom almost died. Then my sister was in a white dress and looked pure. She was with a little boy at her side.

7-17-05 My stepson's daughter would have problems with her first child. I called my stepson and he said she had trouble with the baby.

12-23-09 I saw a beautiful card with a ribbon in it. All it said on the card was Little One. When we were in the restaurant business, he always forgot my name so he always called me "little one."

My sister had called to tell me Beaver died. I used to go out with him. She said he committed suicide. About three weeks later, he came to me in a dream. He was very beautiful with a white light around him and blue light. He said someone had a gun to his head, but what he meant the job he had he was being pressured. Three months later, he came back to me and said everything is ok.

CHAPTER 11

Poems

Before my mom's energy ran out, she said she saw a river and I asked her if it was beautiful. She said. Yes. She said no little girls have to float, that she was building a ship. But did not know what way to go. She said she put four crows on the north, south, east and west, so she would know.

She talked about her loved ones. I said did you see grandma, my mom's mother. She said no, but she saw Uncle Joe, her mother's brother and said she never knew her grandma. She said Uncle Joe was sitting with her. He left but he would be back. My mother was so full of beauty while we were talking and she was talking to her loved ones in the spirit world. I asked here if she was ready to go home to God, Grandma. She said NO! She said when I do I am going to heaven. I asked her again about her leaving and going home and she said yes. I told her I loved her and thank you. She replied, thank you for everything.

Five days later, right before she left this earth planet, she was deleting everything from the time she was born until she was ready to leave. You could hear bits and pieces but more like mumbling the worlds. One time she told my sister she was going to practice.

Leaving and coming back, I asked her if she was ready to leave. She said, "Yes." She passed on.

I had a wart on the bottom of my foot for three years. I had three different doctors say they will get rid of it. The morning my mom passed away, when the nurse said she just took her last breath I stood up. This energy came over me and I knew the wart was gone, and it was. I was just holding on to something. Maybe all the time I was with my mom, when she was in the hospital and whatever went through, because my parents were the best parents in this world and very loving and understanding.

My mom always wrote poems. I got a letter in the mail for poems. I told my mom. She said you write one. So Mother's Day was soon to be and I wrote words here and there. Three months later I found that people for the contest and I asked my mom, did you write a poem? She said no. So I sent my Mother's Day poem in and it took the editor's award. So keep telling God to change my life and he did.

I wrote this poem for my mother and other mothers and Mother Earth, as today Mother Earth is in trouble. Mother is a symbol of the heart. An eternal living love. She has nurtured mankind since the beginning of time. Our effort today can save our tomorrow. Let us peacefully celebrate Mother's Day.

My love and prayers are with you and your families.

Love is more than poetry or more than words can say. I see the grace that's in her eyes. She means everything to me. Every good thing she has given to me so please dear Lord, what can I give unto thee except this heart of mine that I offer thee? Even if I see a tear I know it is not fear. She is so kind and gentle, so give her my love to last throughout the year.

I see the sun and moon and stars and every flower, rain. I see her gentle grace and love that always fills the air. When it comes to mothers, she is all of the above and rare. I see her grace and beauty so what more can I say. When it comes to moms, Happy Mother's Day. "A mother's love is the closest to God's Love."

We are love and a place to become the way for you and me. We list at this moment a reflection of what we are. We are unchanging, impartial love and peace.

"You And Me"

Time is changing. The time is coming. I see a change when the planets move and the trumpets sound. God's will on earth and peace for man will come.

I couldn't let this day go by without calling you just to say Hi.

"Let there Be Light"

I saw the clouds dark and gray. I see the lightning strike. I hear the rolling thunder, and then it starts to rain. The dark turned into night. The morning came. The sun came out and God let it be light.

"My Memory"

There is nothing wrong with your memory. It's just that you let other thoughts get in the way. We should live righteously, divinely, in grace with dignity so we can find inner peace.

Laugh, this is the purpose in life. Shine and lift burdens that will go away. Just forgive and do your best. Life is just a lease on life and space.

Secure your tomorrow. It's time for Nations to come together to greet God.

Grandmas are like coaches. They sit on the sideline and see all.

When I wake today I know it is going to be a beautiful day.

We all have freedom to be free as we see the eagles soaring from tree to tree.

These thoughts I have are not from me but from our father's world to show you that our father loves us more than you will ever know.

"I Hear You"

I heard you call me. Your voice was loud and clear. When I turned around you were never there.

Love is powerful. Love is not just a word or how it comes across. Its how you use it. Love is the best teacher. That's why it's called love.

It is God's love that loves man, not man's love.

"My Soul"

God made me special that I know. It came from up above. He loves me more than I'll ever know. My father's thoughts have touched my soul.

"Today"

Today and every day were made for you and me. You have the power within you to be what you want to be.

"My Mother"

My mother always told me when I was growing up to always read the Good Book and I would find the one I love.

When I sit and meditate I always pray to God that he is always listening and he\ can read my thoughts.

"My Mom"

My mother used to dress me and that's the way I would stay. I always looked so funny. Now I dress that way.

"For You"

I love you very much for all that you have done for me. Now you are with God and mom is still with me. "Happy Father's Day."

"My Sister"

I looked up at my sister as she was looking down at me. What was I doing? I said writing poetry.

"Everything Comes to Pass"

Now the floods are gone. It makes you want to think to only keep what you need and always keep the faith.

"Reflections"

I see the love that fills the air in every face I see. When I look at someone else, it's a reflection of me.

"Dancing in the Sun"

The sun shines on the water, it sprinkles with delight at it dances on the water in the dark moonlight.

"Freedom"

I see the sunlight through the trees. I feel nature's gentle breeze. God made this universe for you and me. He gave us the freedom to be free.

"See Yourself"

My faith is coming through me. With all these beautiful thoughts, he is telling man to see himself, as God or this world will be lost.

"Future"

I see the future where no man has ever been. I sit here waiting and Praying God will take my hand.

"I Am Free"

Today I am thirty. Today I am free to thank myself for being me.

"Loving You"

Everything I say and everything I do it doesn't come from a book. It comes from loving you.

"Laughter"

Having success and prosperity and having a positive life will always bring laughter into my life.

"Stars"

The stars are not just diamonds in the sky. They are full of love and dance with joy. They twinkle; they're bright and big. Now I know this world is big.

"Angels"

Angels don't have wings like butterflies or birds, but are God's thoughts coming to us to fill our hearts with cheer,

"Visualize"

Close your eyes and visualize where you want to be. Open your eyes and keep those thoughts and you will be set free.

"I Know You Love Me"

I'm with you always. Yes I love you. You are there, I'm here. I feel your live that's in the air.

We have the freedom to be free. We're two free spirits God set free to come and go whenever we please.

My love for you is very deep to have the courage to complete.

My love for you is everywhere that fills the sky above. See the love that's in your eyes. Some day we will be one.

I can't conceal in my eyes the love for you that never dies.

My thoughts are with you everywhere. My love for you I'll always have.

God gave me this love to give to you. My love for you I cannot leave.

My love for you will always be for now throughout eternity. Our path in life is free.

"My Dream"

I saw him coming in a dream. He is near, walking toward me, his clothes flowing, and the light around him glowing. He kept coming toward me. He dispersed the thoughts I have of him. He will soon be here. 8-17-97

"You Are Beautiful"

You are beautiful. All your life you did for others. Sometimes there was despair, but in your heart you knew better the love for others was always there.

"Birth"

Life isn't that bad so don't complain. You took birth on this earth planet. Live it out or you will come back to live again and again.

"Smile"

When you look at life, what do I see? I see God filling every space with love that keeps surrounding me. Then I smile back at God and He smiles back at me.

"Nature Turning"

The trees are turning. The birds are chirping. Mother nature's flowers are turning. The winds are coming. The skies are changing to let us know winter is coming.

I thought one day what life would be, I saw all the signs pointing at me.

As love flows from every heart I see it's time to do my part.

Now is the time to let peace flow from every heart.

Every good thing comes from above. Every good thing comes from God. It's time for peace, time for joy. God only made good, so there is no time to cry.

"Shadows"

When you walk on the path of life and see the shadows of light with every step along the way, bestows the grace that can turn this world your way.

"Only God"

Only God can make your dreams come true.
Only God can make the waters blue.
Only God can turn the night to day.
Only God can keep you safe each day.
Only God can free you from a fall.

Only God can make the heaven above and fill every space with love.
Only God can hold your hand.
Only God can understand.

"Treasures"

Only what we can fulfill and walk in the right direction. When we look our where our treasures are and where our hearts are going.

"My Purpose in Life"

I'm full of grace, peace and love that always come my way, the purpose for being and know my purpose is here.

"Grace"

The love and air we breathe is a fragrance that comes from above. God unites us with his love. It gives us growth in grace and patience every day. He gives us meekness, joy and illuminates our way.

"Autumn"

I see a change from spring to autumn. The leaves are falling with every breath I take. The butterflies are leaving with their gentle grace. They'll be back next year to bloom and fly in the air.

"Count Your Blessings"

Did you count your blessings and know that they were true?
Did you find peace in your heart?
Did you keep the faith and say I love you?

"Be Mine"

I am just a soul in love with you, so will you be mind and always be my Valentine?

"Two Birthdays"

I only have two birthdays to celebrate—the time I was born and when I die.

"A Cause"

Everyone is fighting for a cause. The only cause should be God.

"Winter"

It started to rain, then started to freeze and left the ice on the trees. The sun reflected on the ice. It was possible Jack Frost was out for the night.

"I Can't Sleep"

When I went to bed and could not sleep, I started changing God's name instead of sheep.

"Plant a Seed"

Plant a seed and watch yourself grow. You can become as strong as a tree and everything else will unfold.

"Reflections of Life"

God is love and we reflect that love. The clouds above my earth me, the earth beneath my feet. The air that surrounds me, the beauty within me.

"Courage"

God give us the courage to confess the wrong that we have done, or harm we brought to everyone.

Give us the strength and courage to be free and love others as you love me.

"Good Morning"

When you woke us this morning did you do what you had to do?
Did you love one another and make sure you knew the truth?
Did you look at someone else and feel the way they do?

"Nature"

When I think of nature, this is what I see:
I see the birds that build their nests as the deer run through the trees.
I see the chipmunks run around and feed their hungry cheeks.
I see the sunlight through the trees. I feel nature's gentle breeze.
God made this universe for you and me. He gave us the freedom
to be free.

"Heaven"

Heaven is not in the sky or beyond the sea. Heaven is right here
with you and me.

"Keep the Courage"

If you should falter and be discouraged take up the cross and keep
the courage.

"Obstacles"

If obstacles get in your way, only let go to know that God is really
near. His love will cast out all your fears.

"To Hear You"

It's always nice to hear your voice for what you have to say. Your
words are sweet and full of love that makes a perfect day.

"Look at Me"

Look at me. What do you see? I only see the good in you and me.

"Timeless"

Age is timeless and you are great. As you grow in grace you'll see God face to face. So think of God's name with every breath you take.

He watches over us. Until we revise this world so we can all be free, there will be light, love and peace. No more tears, no more fear, no more doubt. He will whisper in our ear, I love You. He will set us free from a world of delusion that can never harm me. Open your heart and let the love pour out for all the word to see.

"Light"

Be he light. Be filled with the light as we are the light of the world.

"Wake Up"

When we wake up we will see this world is only a dream.

"Peace"

Love and peace become the way as false beliefs dissolve for all the human race.

"Space"

We are love. We exist at this moment. Now we are a reflection of what we see. As love flows from every heart, we are unchanging emotional love of peace.

"Health"

Fashion every flower. Fashion every weed. Death is more beautiful than the human eye can see.

"My Mom"

I know my mom is with me. I feel her presence each day. I believe she's telling me to go on with my life, to know what she went through, and to guide me with her life. The day will come when she can rest to know that I did my best.

"Forgive"

This is the time for forgiveness. We are the light of the world. All it takes you and me to see this world free. God made the hills and sandy roads for us to walk upon. We must respect the thing he made or soon it will be gone. I see the future where man has never been. My father is coming through me with all these beautiful thoughts. He is telling man to see himself, as God or this world will be lost.

"Sister Dear"
Sister dear, I love you so. You left this world without a tear.
You gave so much. Now you are gone.
Your love for life will carry on.
You opened your eyes of blue to see one more time. You took two breaths and left. With grace and love and dignity God gave you his grace, his love and might. Now you are in the light. I see your face as it shines. You will come again one more time.

"Edgar Cayce"

God made us special that I know it came from up above. He loves us more than we will ever know.
Edgar Cayce's thoughts have touched my soul.

CHAPTER 12

Create A Positive Life

Wake Up To Your Own Inner Courage

When you wake in the morning and throughout the day repeat some sayings t keep you uplifted.

Transform your thoughts and life completely. Think well of yourself and others. God has given us the sword of reason which we can use to free ourselves from this world of delusion. But apply that God-given power of discrimination to choose right action in preference to wrong action. To be mentally above your troubles.

Just know and believe in your heart. Think of God planting love in your heart day and night. Using your own spiritual effort so you can remove the veil of ignorance from your consciousness.

Honor yourself

Respect yourself.

Meditate upon yourself

Kneel to your self as God dwells within you as you.

Surrender yourself with the protective force of love and peace and harmony. Resolve and eliminate and repel negative influences from any source. Think of a powerful brilliant aura that repels negativity. Tremendous peace and love surround me.

Enhance your natural ability to receive psychic impressions, insights and information about yourself and others.

Know psychic impressions come to me easily. I am a natural channel of universal insights and wisdom. I am more psychic every day. I have powerful psychic ability are mind.

Man walks in the direction which he looks and where his treasures are. They're where his heart is.

Everything spiritual comes from above.

Know the truth about yourself and all your actions will bear fruit.

When you get good thoughts those are angel thoughts passing from God to man.

Don't go through life with blinders on.

Don't put weight on your heart. Relax or it will make the situation worse.

However things go you must remain calm, quiet and peaceful that peace is the source of prosperity. Self-containment is the act of prosperity and it is the highest spiritual strength. There is nothing to match it.

Smile

Thee is an ocean of love within all of us. The love of God is so pure. It is unconditional. It is always there if you allow to drink this love. Even if you make even a simple effort you can experience this love. Allow this understanding take you higher and higher. Make it more and more divine.

Trust Yourself

Believe in that which is not, in order that it may be the imaginations he creative power in our hands. Everything in which we have faith succeeds.

Just as miracles happen through slow motion exercises.

> Give all your problems to God
> God will guide you moment by moment
> Be grateful for your knowledge
> O sun, let my lost strength be restarted
> We are aware of the universe.

In the Aquarium you don't pray. You should ask God to pray for you.

We are only on a journey going through a planetary shift.

You can meditate to help those who are suffering. Think of them in your prayers.

If you have a sick mind it will cause sick organs. You will suffer only think well of people or they will not heal.

Always be grateful for the beauty around you.

Poor indeed is he who does not show anger, but worse indeed is he who cannot control it in himself. And there most fail. Though often those who flare up quickly, also forgive quickly. It remains as a little children asking, seeking, living. Guide thou me O God in the steps I take, in the words I say day by day.

By letting go it all gets done. The word is won by those who let go. But when you try and try, it is even to be on the winning.

I think of this world as a beautiful garden and every one in it a flower.

Inner wealth is called the heart.

Surrender to one's own self. The greater the self, the higher self.

Wrap your problems in a bundle and give it to God.

Turn within the force behind your actions and thoughts with faith. You become free in the world.

When you do good, that good comes from the God within you.

Don't doubt. Magnetize it. Let it come to you

Right is right. Wrong is wrong.

If you want to criticize someone, look in the mirror. Thank yourself.

In the beginning

In the beginning God

God created the heaven and earth.

Then there was light.

Now is the time of the new beginning. As God Will of God is expressed on Earth With the Understanding of light, love peace. We should all do our part. A God dwells in you as you for God is all in all.

Open up your heart and the pure presence of Unconditional Love pours out. Know you are one with the light. Filled with the light. Illumined by its Light. You are the light of the world.

Send forth that light. Merge with this light. We are the light of the world.

There is one Light of Love Peace and Understanding. It's moving across the face of the Earth, touching and illuminating every soul.

All kingdoms of the earth will respond. And the planet will be alive with Light and Love, peace and understanding. It is moving across the face of the Earth, touching and illuminating every soul.

All kingdom of the earth will respond. And the planet is alive with Light and Love.

With total oneness let love flow from every heart. Forgiveness begins in every soul.

Now from the light of the world, there is once presence and power of the Universe. God is healing and harmonizing Planet Earth.

Create inner peace. Listen to music. Think of gentle winds, tropical oceans.

There are challenges to our creativity. If you want an abundance of fortuitous opportunities into your life, said, "I feel lucky today. I have incredibly good luck. My positive dreams are becoming my reality. I attract harmony and good luck. There is a steady flow of good luck into my life."

Everything in the past died yesterday. Everything in the future was born today.

The greatest enemy is the self if you don't accept the self.

Control time. Don't let it control you. Set objectives and establish priorities to create extra hours in the day.

Know your enthusiastic setting daily goals. Feel great satisfaction when you accomplish your goals. Just stay on course and reach your goals. This is good for children too.

Look at God in everything.

Know you are a self-starter and enjoy getting things done.

Look at the good in people.

Set your affections on things above, not on earth or who we are, the expression of unchanging love and divine wisdom.

Be a free thinker.

Release the flow of creative ideas in your mind. Know you have a great creative genie within you.

Angels are God's thoughts passing to man.

"If you get an angel thought, Nurture your creativity into expression. And you do not lack ideas. Know you are filled with inspiration.

Whatever is possible to God is possible for you to accomplish wit His help."

Stand your ground with truth and love and you will win.

God's will is that you remain free. Be a free thinker.

Forgive yourself and your past.

Remove the veil of ignorance from your consciousness.

Keep your thoughts free from thinking about illnesses.

Know that all your channels are filled with truth and love.'

If you have a problem or pain, Zap it out right away.

If you cater to your children you will lose them. If you do not give values you expand the ego to such an extent that there is nothing to stop it. Then their life becomes nothing to stop it. Then their life becomes destructive, and then the child will disobey parents and leave the home.

When you see wrong and start right. That is called the flow, continuity of life. Just accept the wrong and try to do it right,

Don't believe that wrong has to be punished, or to lock up a person or kill him.

Every day say to yourself, "I shall live this day with grace." If you keep complaining about your job and environment it will bring misery. Compliments bring strength.

It is our birthright to be happy but if you do not seek discipline you will never be happy,

By meditating we take our garbage out.

When you have spiritual powers you sine like the sun.

Just as people have more faith in the material things than spiritual, it's because they have separated themselves from God.

If you let the senses control you it will take over and it will win.

When your health becomes bad, change negative thoughts to positive right away. Don't exchange one disease for another.

All addictions come from the same source, promising satisfaction.

Don't lose your identity.

We are all children of God and sometimes we get off track.

Putting stress and limitations on yourself stops the flow of circulation, just as anxiety. It will cause the body illness and diseases.

Don't hang on to your problems or they will just get bigger and bigger. Drop the problem right away.

Have faith and trust in God and he will take care of it in his own way.

The mind is very powerful. If you think it, you can do it.

Sometimes "you" give people the power to hurt you. Change your negative thoughts to positive right away before the problem gets out of hand. Then you yourself can't handle it.

Don't waste your energy on others.

You picked this life and you have to live it out. Or your lessons will just get tougher.

If you have odds with someone, bless them. Inhale your love to them and send your love to them a few days and you will feel better.

Don't have idols. You will lose your true identity of who you really are.

Be careful who you pick for your friends. They reflect you and you reflect them.

What we breathe in just for today. Just for today let go of anger and worry. Count your blessings, live honestly and be kind to all living things.

If you want to judge others, judge yourself first.

"Those who are grateful always become great, full of wealth and prosperity. May this be your path."

We are the light of the world.

It isn't what goes into the mouth. It's what comes out of the mouth.

It isn't what we eat. It is what we eat mentally.

If you have a stirring within you listen to God for his ideas to be filled with his inspiration and express it in a creative way. Whatever is possible for God is possible to accomplish with his help.

Fill yourself with healing, love and energy. Adapt to life change. All things will work together.

Work out your own salvation.

Free yourself of guilt or blaming yourself or others. Enjoy a new life with love, kindness and acceptance. Forgive and release yourself of all guilt. There is a sense of peace and tranquility about yourself. Keep positive loving thoughts and memories. Free yourself from condemnation and guilt. Know and dissolved and gone. Start each day with a clean slate.

Do something positive with your life.

Snap out of the way you feel.

Repeat: I have tremendous willpower and I can accomplish anything I set my mind to. I am a powerhouse of determination. My mind is made up nothing can deter me. I have a strong determination to succeed.

Release the knowledge in your subconscious that you have a strong and powerful memory. Know it is easy to remember desired information, that now it is easy to remember desired information. You have complete confidence in your ability that your memories will rise effortlessly o the surface.

"Work out your own salvation."

With your imagination don't let your energy go backwards. Go forward and change evil thoughts to spiritual. Have faith.

Whatever happens remain in control, tranquil and serene. Regardless of the circumstances. Be a patient person. Grow more patient and understand every day. Let it surround you. Be relaxed, calm and at ease. Automatically become calm under stress.

Let fears and worry dissolve from your life. Radiate faith, belief and confidence in yourself. Today know you are free of fear and worry. Replace negative thoughts with positive ones. Know you are calm, confident and secure.

You will see the salvation of the planet before your eyes. Separation is no more. The healing has taken place. The world is restored to sanity. This is the beginning of peace on Earth Good Will toward all. Let the Love flow from every heart, forgiveness reign in every soul, all hearts and minds are one in perfect understanding.

It is done And it is so.

When you cry you're alone. When you smile, everyone will smile.

Using your subconscious mind, relieve physical, mental and emotional trauma. Positive healing energy flows through me. A body heals quickly and totally. A blazing healing light energy dissolves any affliction from me. Know you are now filled with wholeness, health and perfection.

Work out your own salvation.

God has only good in store for you. Don't let fear get in the way. Don't live in darkness as HATE blinds the mind in jealousy.

Everyone comes into this world carrying a bag of his own destiny. Whatever is put in you is what you have to eat.

When life dances in front of you it is a gift from God. Different times is a gift from God. Sometime we are being tested. My path in life is free and never separate myself from God.

Food sustains the life of man and then you hear that food can kill man.

CHAPTER 13

The Author

I hope this book will change your life before 2012. Edgar Cayce was a big part of my life and still is, as he was a great prophet and psychic. As the river never stops flowing your energy can flow through yoga and meditation.

Not to be modest, here is something about the author. Gayle says God is the real author. He is in control.

Gayle is a self-realized spiritual person. She has a strong bond with herself. She looks at life with light and love through her eyes. She has dedicated her life to God and to others. She says you are nothing less than light and love.

She taught herself in many ways. Gayle is a yoga instructor of 45 years, volunteers at many places. She got special commendation awards in recognition of significant contributions to community life in Wisconsin.

She has been on national TV for another book she wrote and donated it to the Edgar Cayce A.R.E Clinic foundation and the library. She had the best parents in the world. She is an activist in her community. She does public relations for the K. G designs and is an associate with Milton Billoch, who is formerly of the Platters.

She has written poems that got published and one took the editor's award, "It Was a Mother's Day Poem."

She would like to write a book on yoga. She is writing a true story based on Joseph and the amazing Technicolor Dream coat. It is about love and forgiveness.

She was hoping her friend would do a movie on it, like the Deep Blue Sea, and her friend's song would be a number one hit for her story. Her missions never end. She looks at others with her spiritual eye, not the physical eye.

She knew nine months before husband died that great things were going to happen in her life. She feels the angel and others in the spiritual world are always with her and guiding her. She hopes everyone will be as blessed as she is.

She says God is the real author and planned her life. Now it is time for it to unfold.

When you are spiritual you shine like the sun and know all. It is time to see God in each other and in yourself. I hope this book will help people make the right decision before the new kingdom comes. As she is a self realized spiritual person.

New identity emerges from religious arena.

There are many voices in the spiritual arena clamoring for political action. But people whose spirituality is only personal to them often have difficulty finding an outlet for their spiritual inclinations. This is a new voice making her way.

She encourages us to develop our spiritual inclinations and serves as a guide toward our own spiritual possibilities.

Wake up. The end is near. The book is based only on thought. There is no exception to who can benefit from personal spirituality. Don't condemn others. Instead bless them from the lord God of your being. Inhale your love from them and send your love to them. You will feel better and they will have something good to say to you.

Know the truth about yourself. We are the light of the world and only we can restore this world back to sanity. This is the way to peace on earth for all, so let your love flow from every heart and forgiveness in your soul.

Everything is a state of mind. Everything comes from within. The mind is very powerful. Don't limit yourself. In God's eyes we are all special. Life is a test and we are all being tested.

Bless your enemies and God will surely come looking for you.

Avoid people if someone challenges you of excellence, elegance and grace.

Nothing is wrong in this world if you don't hate someone or create a superiority complex, or make someone else feel inferior.

Change your negative thoughts into positive ones. Start living every day with grace and love. Anything that was impossible, make that task possible.

If you ever read Edgar Cayce's book, I'm sure you saw where to spend time in meditation. As Edgar Cayce called it the "Magic Silence." How easy to achieve twenty minutes in the morning and evening. I can add much to the quality of life.

Psalm 46 to focus your mind and inspire your soul.

We were born to help each other, not kill each other. Everything in God's world is perfect.

Don't change the world. Change yourself.

We are on a journey going through a planetary shift. In the beginning God. God created the heaven and the earth and said there be light. Now is the time for a new beginning.

It is a new Heaven that comes. It is the Kingdom of light, love, peace and Understanding. What is true of me is true of everyone, to let the pure essence of Unconditional Love pour out.

I am one with the light, filled with the light, illuminated by the light. I am the light of this world.

Our purpose is to send forth the light. As the light of the world, Peace and Understanding is moving. It flows across the face of the Earth, touching and illuminating every soul in the shadow of the illusion. Darkness is now the light of Reality.

Let mankind be returned to Godkind. Let love flow from every heart, forgiveness reign in every soul. God is healing and harmonizing Planet Earth. All false beliefs and error patterns are dissolved. The sense of separation is no more; the healing has taken place and the world restored to sanity. Pray on Earth God's Will toward all. Let love flow from every heart, forgiveness, reigns in every soul. All hearts and minds are on in perfect understanding.

Love and support our troops. You were called upon it's your duty to fight this war, to serve in every way, a war you did not start. When your duty was performed the gift of reward of the government turned you down. So who do you fight, to start another war? You refused for a ware you did not start. Brave as you were, money cannot bring back our men and women who died for a cause. Now is the time to fight for your rights or our government will be lost.

A country cannot prosper without a people kind or a constitutional head to guide it.

We can stop this war today. We can stop this way with love. We can win everyday every war from shore to shore. We can get down on our knees and pray. God will speed our love for the whole universe to see.

Without love we have nothing. Where there was darkness there will be light. Sometimes our senses are lost in sight. I believe we will always be free, so the planet is alive with light, love and peace.

In every mind and heart will being so the world is restored of peace on earth with god's will toward all to see.

Let the love flow from every heart with light, love and peace and understanding. We can open our hearts and let the love pour out to every man, woman and child. This is the time for forgiveness.

We are the light of the world. All it takes is you and I to see this world back to sanity. God made the hills and sandy roads for us to walk upon. We must respect the things he made or soon it will all be gone.

I've seen the future where man has never been. MY father is coming through telling man to see himself as God or this world will be lost.

A Woman of Strength

A strong woman works out every day to keep her body in shape . . . but a woman of strength kneels in prayer to keep her soul in shape . . .

A strong woman isn't afraid of anything . . . but a woman of strength shows courage in the midst of her fear . . .

A strong woman won't let anyone get the best of her . . . but a woman of strength gives the best of herself to everyone . . .

A strong woman makes mistakes and avoids the same in the future . . . a woman of strength realizes life's mistakes can also be blessings and capitalizes on them . . .

A strong woman walks sure footedly . . . but a woman of strength knows God will catch her when she falls . . .

A strong woman wears the look of confidence on her face . . . but a woman of strength wears grace . . .

A strong woman has faith that she is strong enough for the journey . . . but a woman of strength has faith that it is in the journey that she will become strong.

-Anonymous

I always whispered a prayer in his ear each night that whatever they need will come to them. Always be the one with God and me on our lips until your last breath; that he would have the connection to do it.

Pray for your children. Think of them having a radiant body and they will get energy from it. Whisper to them when they go to bed to become one with God. So no matter what challenges he faces, he would have that connection is to carry him through it.

Thank you for reading this book. I hope it will help you to lead a more powerful exciting life.

Remember you can heal yourself in the Aquarian Age. Self-healing is the process of relationship between the Infinite power of the soul. It is from a state of compassion, of compassion meditation, that the healing activity of God within the being flows. We are nothing without God. Never underestimate the power of God.

Self-healing is the genuine process of relationship between the physical and the infinite power of the soul. A state of compassion, meditation, the healing of God within the being flows.

Thoughts become feelings. Then they become emotions. Then that becomes desires. Then that becomes neuroses. The mistakes you make occur because you are attached to your emotions and you lose your good judgment. "Let Your Ego Go."

When selfishness and conceit go away peace comes and the mind and body are healed. Then you will forever be healthy. O Mind, think well of yourself and others.

Remembering the One God in meditation, all diseases are healed. Only constant remembering of your true identity brings true health.

I will always think of Edgar Cayce as a great being and this world an ocean of joy.

Stay on a spiritual path, change your beliefs now. Forgive the past.

Wake up and you will see this world is only an illusion, only a dream.

As all my thoughts come from God.

May God bless America. May God bless this world. Let Us Sing God Bless America.

NAMEASTE
From My Heart To Your Heart With Great Respect and Love
Gayle